THE SKEGNESS DATE BOOK
1850 - 2000

C 1900

Skegness Town Council
2006

Published by   Skegness Town Council, Town Hall, Skegness, Lincolnshire

Copyright ©   Winston Kime.

All rights reserved. No part of this publication may be reproduced, stored in a retrievable system or transmitted in any form or by any means without permission of the copyright holder.

ISBN 0-9554820-0-3
ISBN 978-0-9554820-0-7

First published 2006.

With best wishes.

Winston Kime

Front cover:
Skegness central beach near the beginning of the twentieth century, with Farmer's Tearooms, fairground swings with other rides and a shellfish barrow. The paddle-steamer, Privateer is just leaving the pierhead landing-stage for a trip across the Wash to Hunstanton. (Photo: F.S.W.Major Collection.)

CONTENTS.

Foreword.	4
Introduction.	5
Skegness Events, 1850-2000.	6
The Jolly Fisherman.	77
Population , 1801-2001.	78
Street Maps.	79
Council Chairmen and Town Mayors.	88
Skegness Town Clerks	89
Skegness Town Council	90
Honoured Citizens and Jolly Fisherman Statuettes.	90
Skegness Councils in pictures.	91
Council Offices and Town Halls.	94
Index.	96

FOREWORD

By Councillor Phil Kemp, Town Mayor of Skegness, 2006-07.

Once again, renowned local historian Winston Kime has produced a book about historical aspects of Skegness and the area. This time he has written about a period of 150 years covering the notable events of Skegness, giving us an insight into local prominent personalities and the visits of important people to the Town. With a selection of topical photographs, the book is well constructed and a joy to read.

Whether you wish to just flick through photographs, read selected items or pore over the pages from cover to cover, it is a book that will appeal to all ages and from all walks of life. It is a celebration of Skegness and another valuable edition chronicling historical events that have helped shape our town.

As you look through the pages, you may well be intrigued with some of the events and the personalities involved. You may well come across references to family members of days gone by and even see some of your ancestors in the photographs, so a real study of the book is very worthwhile. In this way, you could find a personal significance to the book above that which is mere historical fact.

It is my privilege to commend to you a book that brings to life events and people in a way that grasps readers' attention. This is one of the familiar trademarks of Winston Kime's writings and this book will not disappoint. So please read, study, scrutinise and most of all, thoroughly enjoy the latest addition to the family of books so carefully prepared and produced.

c 1905

INTRODUCTION.

Skegness goes back to Viking times, as its name implies -Skeggi's ness, or headland - a landing of those fierce warriors in the great invasion of the ninth century. Even before that there was a Roman road from Lincoln to Skegness, but those distant days and its subsequent history as a small trading port have been described in other publications and the present record deals only with the rise of Skegness as a seaside resort.

The information contained in the following pages has been accumulated over the years from many different sources. It is hoped that it will be a useful reference and also a book to dip into or read through, perhaps reviving a few memories for those who have a long acquaintance with the area, as well as interesting others wishing to learn more about it.

Space, as well as the pitfalls of selection, have prevented me including the deaths and achievements of prominent residents, except in a few cases where they have achieved national fame. Whilst I have endeavoured to obtain dates and basic information relating to the town's many varied organisations there are some about which no facts have been forthcoming and possibly others that have been overlooked, for which I apologise.

Some important happenings have to be left out because, by their very nature, they are too numerous to record here; as an instance, the scores of notable rescues carried out by Skegness lifeboats. These events are described elsewhere, in some cases in my own work. Space and cost also rules out all but a handful of illustrations, but again, there are other books devoted mainly to old pictures of the town

Many years ago I discovered The Date Book for Lincoln and Neighbourhood from the Earliest Times to the Present, published in Lincoln in 1866. The author's name was not disclosed, but he is believed to have been a Lincoln journalist employed by The Lincolnshire, Rutland and Stamford Mercury, launched as The Stamford Mercury in that town in 1695. The Lincoln Date Book, as it is usually referred to, has been a little downgraded by some county historians because entries are not individually sourced, which would have been a very difficult undertaking and tedious to the general reader for whom it was intended. It was undoubtedly a most interesting compendium for a great number of readers over a long period of time and I shall be very happy if the present work generates a fraction of that attention. I would think it a useful thing if every town compiled a Date Book of its own.

There may be some errors, and certainly some omissions in the following pages and perhaps readers will draw them to the attention of the publisher so that, should there ever be another edition, the oversights can be corrected or made good. I am very grateful to all the people and organisations, and not least the Town Council, who have provided information and other assistance enabling this work to be published. I must also thank Skegness Civic Society and RACol for their financial contributions.
Without their help publication would not have been possible.

Winston Kime.

Skegness. 2006.

SKEGNESS EVENTS, 1850-2000.

1850-56 WHITE'S LINCOLNSHIRE DIRECTORY, 1856, states that Skegness 'until lately an obscure village, is rising in celebrity, both as a bathing-place and a port, upwards of 6000 tons of coals being landed here in one summer.' The coal was dumped on the beach by colliers from Tyneside and carted to a coal yard in the area of what is now Tower Gardens The village had had a number of private lodging houses and two 'large and commodious hotels,' both providing warm and cold seawater baths and about 30 beds. Richard Millson was landlord of the Vine and Sarah Hildred at the New Hotel (later Hildreds). There were bathing machines for the visitors, but not much else except miles of firm sands and the bracing sea air. The lifeboat was kept close to the beach and in the great storm of 30 August 1833 the crew saved ten lives, although about twenty more bodies were washed ashore.

Lord Monson was lord of the manor, but the greater part of the soil belonged to the Earl of Scarbrough, the heirs of C.B.Massingberd and to Charles Reynardson. The small church of St. Clement's was in the patronage of Lord Scarbrough and the absentee rector lived in Hampshire. There was a Wesleyan Methodist Chapel in High Street, built in 1848, and a small free school(opened in 1839) on Roman Bank, supported by subscriptions and taught by Charles and Ann Harrison. Thomas Almond had a temperance hotel in the High Street and also kept the Post Office. There was a grocer and draper, a tailor, 2 shoemakers, a coalmerchant, 3 blacksmiths and a wheelwright. The inhabitants numbered 366, in 1851.

Winthorpe was a separate parish with 299 inhabitants, Lord Monson being lord of the manor, as at Skegness and the land was divided between a number of small owners. The parish church of St. Mary's was built in the perpendicular style, whilst the vicarage was consolidated with that of Burgh-le-Marsh. The Ship Hotel, kept by Thomas Hutton, stood on Roman Bank at its junction with Burgh Road. (The two roads roughly marked the boundaries between Winthorpe and Skegness.) Winthorpe also had two beerhouses, a shop and a coalmerchant. Atkin Moody, the carrier, took passengers and goods to Spilsby market every Monday. There were a number of farmers and graziers in both parishes.

LIFEBOAT. The first lifeboat on the Lincolnshire coast was stationed at Gibraltar Point in October 1825 by the Lincolnshire Coast Shipwreck Association. The station was moved to Skegness in 1830, in charge of Coxswain Samuel Moody who held the post for over forty years (1830-71), being awarded two silver medals for bravery during that period. As early as 1816, a 24-pounder brass mortar for firing lifelines from the shore had been established at Skegness on the recommendation of its inventor, Captain George Manby, after a survey of the whole coast.

1851   CHURCH ATTENDANCE. A Census of Religious Worship in 1851 has been described as a unique venture in British statistical history and was taken at the same time as the 1851 census of population. The returns were compiled by the minister or other official of the church in each denomination in every locality. The returns for Skegness and Winthorpe gave the following information:

St. Clement's Church.
    Usual attendance at Morning service, 'about 40.'
    Sunday school, 'about 90.'

Wesleyan Methodist Chapel (erected 1848).
    Afternoon service. Average for previous twelve months, 40
    Evening service. ditto. 75

Primitive Methodist Chapel (erected 1836).
    Afternoon service, 54
    Evening service, 46

St.Mary's Church, Winthorpe.
    Usual attendance at afternoon service, 'about 50.'

(Information from Lincolnshire Returns of the Census of Religious Worship, 1851, compiled by R.W.Ambler, MA. and published in 1979 by Lincoln Record Society. Reproduced by kind permission of the publisher.)

1858   CURATE TO BISHOP. Rev. Edward Steere moved to Skegness as curate and afterwards became Bishop of Central Africa, building a cathedral in Zanzibar on the site of the old slave market. He died there in 1882, aged 54, and was buried in his cathedral.

1859   COASTGUARD STATION at Gibraltar Point came into service, at that time being close to the waterside; the building still remains as part of the nature reserve.

1862   SEA VIEW HOTEL erected and opened by Hobson Dunkley, Grimsby builder, with his daughter as manager.

1864   SHIPWRECK ASSOCIATION. At a meeting in Spilsby on January 11, the Lincolnshire Coast Shipwreck Association, finding itself in financial difficulties, agreed to transfer its operation and assets to the Royal National Lifeboat Institution, resulting in new investment for the four Lincolnshire stations. Skegness received a new and larger lifeboat that same year and the South Parade boathouse was rebuilt to accommodate it.

HERBERT INGRAM. The new Skegness lifeboat was received in October, replacing the aged vessel which had been in use for almost forty years. The new boat was paid for by the widow of Boston MP, Herbert Ingram, in memory of her husband who had drowned with their eldest son in a shipping collision on Lake Michigan in 1860. Ingram, a native of Boston, founded the Illustrated London News - still circulating - in 1842 and he is also commemorated with a fine statue in Boston marketplace.

The Herbert Ingram lifeboat was in service at Skegness, 1864-74, followed by a second boat of the same name, also provided by Mrs. Ingram, which served until 1888.

1865   WINTHORPE SCHOOL, close to St.Mary's Church, built at a cost of £150 and opened with twenty-year-old Mary Epton in charge and between 20 and 30 children of all age groups whose attendance fluctuated according to the demands of the land. The school was maintained by government grants and parents' weekly pennies The building is now converted as the Charnwood Tavern.

1867   PARLIAMENTARY FRANCHISE. The Reform Bill of 1867 allowed working men the Parliamentary vote, but only in the towns. Agricultural workers had to wait until 1884 before they were authorised to cast their votes. Women were discounted altogether and had to battle for their rights until the next century.

1870   PIG CLUB. Skegness & District Pig Club formed. Many working men kept a pig and if one died because of disease the club paid out compensation.

1872   SHEEP CLIPPING CONTEST. The Stamford Mercury of June 14 reported that at Burgh Fat Stock Market, Elias and John Hogg of Skegness, sons of Mr Everington's shepherd, won first and second prizes of ten and five shillings in the boys' under 14 sheep clipping contest. The two lads, it was said, 'were so small that it was a matter of wonder that they had been able to shear their sheep'.

WORKHOUSE CHILDEN'S TREAT. A Mercury report of August 23 stated that on Saturday, 'through the kindness of Mr. William Everington of Skegness, a vice chairman of the Board of Guardians, a party of children from the Spilsby Union (workhouse) were taken to the coast for a day of recreation. On arrival at Skegness they were supplied with refreshment and then they departed to the waterside where some pleasant hours were spent before they returned home full of glee.'

1873   RAILWAY extended on the single track from Wainfleet to Skegness, opening for passenger traffic on 28 July, operated by the Great Northern Railway. Skegness station contained four platforms and six sidings.

SHOCKING TRIPPERS. A large train excursion from Lincoln on August 23 brought complaints of a number of bathers of both sexes 'disporting themselves in the nude to shock the modesty of the natives and visitors' and it was feared that this disgusting behaviour would frighten off other visitors.

1876   NEW SKEGNESS. A development plan for the new resort town drawn up for the Earl of Scarbrough by George Booth Walker, Wainfleet surveyor. The construction of Lumley Road began the same year.

WESLEYAN METHODIST CHAPEL opened on 30 July at the west end of High Street on the site of an earlier chapel. Soon after completion, Skegness's population began to soar and plans had to be made to replace it with a larger building.

1877   SKEGNESS PIER COMPANY formed in December under the patronage of the Earl of Scarbrough with capital of £25,000 in five thousand - £5 shares. The directors were H.V.Tippet, the earl's agent, James Martin of Wainfleet Hall, John Mackinder of Lincoln, Colonel Grantham of Spilsby, Edward Charlesworth of Nottingham, John Thimbleby, Spilsby solicitor, Hobson Dunkley of the Sea View Hotel, T.A.Bellamy, Spilsby printer, William Everington, the earl's chief tenant in Skegness, Rev.H.J.Cheales of Friskney and Charles Hildred, a local hotel proprietor. The original plan showed the pier situated opposite the Sea View Hotel.

SKEGNESS STEAM LAUNDRY, Roman Bank, established.

1878   GASWORKS completed at a cost of £3,500 by a local company headed by the Earl of Scarbrough. By the end of the year, 56 street lamps were in place.

PLEASURE GARDENS laid out by S.G. Randall, the Earl of Scarbrough's head gardener. (In the 1920s it was renamed the Tower Gardens.)

1879   SEWERAGE FARM and works completed at Cow Bank when sewers for the new town were laid. The scheme was devised by Durham civil engineer, D.Balfour, costing £6,700, to which Lord Scarbrough contributed £5,000 , the balance being paid by the sanitary authority. The service connections were not finally completed until 1882. The scheme was for land treatment, as opposed to discharge into the sea, ensuring complete cleanliness of the beaches. The site, at the bottom of Richmond Drive, is now a nature reserve.

GRAND PARADE completed, the limestone blocks forming the retaining wall being brought from the Earl of Scarbrough's quarry at Roche Abbey, near Sandbeck House, South Yorkshire.

	PLEASURE GARDENS PAVILION opened for catering and other occasions.

PLEASURE GARDENS PAVILION opened for catering and other occasions.

ST. MATTHEW'S CHURCH foundation stone laid on 5 November by the Countess of Scarbrough.

1880 NATIONAL SCHOOL opened on Roman Bank, at the junction of Ida Road The cost was £1,500, but the Earl of Scarbrough gave the land and contributed £500 to the building fund. There was accommodation for 250 children. Abraham Porter was appointed headmaster and held the post up to his death in 1921.

CRICKET GROUND with pavilion opened in Marsh Lane, shortly afterwards renamed Cricket Ground Lane and eventually Richmond Drive. The cost of laying out the ground and building the pavilion and grandstand was £2,276

ST. MATTHEW'S CHURCH, only partly built, consecrated for services by the Bishop of Lincoln, Christopher Wordsworth.

FIRST RESIDENT RECTOR of Skegness installed in the person of the Rev. Francis Baldwin who came to Skegness from Maltby, Yorks., the vicarage of the Earl of Scarbrough whose home was at nearby Sandbeck Park.

CATTLE MARKET established near railway station with fortnightly sales, but it had only a short life.

LUMLEY HOTEL, Lumley Square opened on Good Friday under management of Matthew Enderby.

WHALE MUSEUM opened in High Street by Thomas Spikin, exhibiting many curiosities, including the skeleton of a whale.

1881 PIER opened on Whit Saturday, June 4, although the buildings at the entrance and at the pierhead were not completed until near the end of the summer. There was no official opening because of the rush to capture the bank holiday income.

PIER HOTEL opened, described in the press' as 'perhaps the most imposing structure in the town.'

DUKE OF EDINBURGH, HRH Prince Alfred, second son of Queen Victoria, landed at the pierhead on August 13, from a launch put out by the steam yacht, Lively, anchored offshore. Being a surprise visit, only a small crowd welcomed him and he was driven in a carriage to inspect the local coastguard and then continued by carriage along the coast, inspecting other coastguard stations before rejoining the yacht at Grimsby. Edinburgh Avenue and Prince Alfred Avenue, off Grand Parade, commemorate the visit.

1881 LION HOTEL opened in March, operated by its builder, Samuel Clarke.

ESTATE OFFICES of the Earl of Scarbrough built on Roman Bank at the north junction of Roman Bank and Algitha Road, costing £3,000, the contractor again Samuel Clarke.

GARFITT'S BANK, the first in Skegness, opened a branch in the Estate Offices. It was later absorbed by the Capital & Counties Bank and later still, by Lloyds Bank.

RAILWAY. The Great Northern Railway Company constructed 'the south curve' near Firsby Junction to avoid excursion trains having to reverse into Firsby station

SHRIMPING ACCIDENT. Boston Guardian of March 26 reported that Skegness fisherman, Henry Moody, had a narrow escape when his shrimping cart entangled with the wreck of a Spanish vessel which had floundered at Skegness forty years earlier. It was visible only at very low water and with the fast incoming tide, Mr. Moody was forced to cut his horse free and abandon the cart and contents to the devouring waves.

FREEMASONS. The opening of the Lumley Lodge was celebrated on April 20 'with a banquet at Brother Hildred's Hotel.'

CYCLING. Skegness Bicycle Club formed at a meeting in the Estate Offices in May.

PIGEON SHOOTING. A pigeon shooting match with live pigeons was held in a paddock at the rear of the Sea View Hotel.

FOOTBALL. Skegness Football Club formed at a public meeting in Hildreds Hotel on October 21. J.B.Ward' was appointed secretary, and C.H.Tippet, treasurer. Farmer William Everington promised to make a field available near the railway station for a playing pitch.

PRIMITIVE METHODISTS opened a new chapel on the west side of Roman Bank just north of School Passage. It seated 60 people and cost £327.

SKEGNESS PARISH MAGAZINE produced in January for the first time. Edited by rector Rev. Francis Baldwin, it mentioned that in 1880 there were 20 burials in the parish, almost half being children under five. There were also 23 baptisms and 6 weddings.

STORM, in October, with gales doing enormous damage all over the county. Warth & Dunkley's 70 foot brickyard chimney was blown down, as well as chimneys on the Lumley and Pier hotels. Bathing machines were overturned and a wooden stables in Alexandra Road was lifted up and carried 30 yards.

TRIPPERS, Sir Charles Anderson, in his Lincoln Pocket Guide, wrote that at Skegness 'the sands are good but the coast flat and ugly. It is chiefly frequented by "trippers" who come by the railway lately opened, from Nottingham and other large towns, to wash and carouse for the day.'

READING ROOM and Library opened at junction of Lumley Road and Rutland Road. A small charge was made for admittance to the Reading Room and the Library contained about 700 books. The amenity was forced to close after only a few years before becoming Hiley's Restaurant, noted for its shilling hot dinners. When the diner eventually closed down the building became the bank presently known as the National-Westminster.

1882 SKEGNESS HERALD, the town's first newspaper, was launched on June 30. Editor and publisher of the weekly was John Avery who printed it at Avery's Steam Printing Works, Lumley Road, now the basement of the National-Westminster Bank.

WESLEYAN METHODISTS vacated their High Street chapel, after only six years, to move to a new and much larger building in Algitha Road, opened on July 13. It provided seating for 600 people and a Sunday School was erected at the rear.

PARISH CONSTABLES. At a meeting of the Parish Vestry in the National School on February 17, the following 12 persons were appointed to serve as constables: James Allen, lodging-house keeper, John Blackburn, carpenter, John Borman, coal agent, Thomas Brown, lodging-house keeper, Joseph Bull, lodging house keeper, Frederick Cartwright, baker, Charles Dixon, lodging house keeper, Edward Lee, blacksmith, George Randall, gardener, George Richardson, saddler and John Riste,

SWIMMING BATHS. Skegness Turkish, Hot & Cold Swimming Baths company formed with capital of £3,000 made up of 600 shares of £5, chaired by the Earl of Scarbrough. - There were separate swimming baths for ladies and gents and seven private baths for each, and also three Turkish baths. Sea water was piped along a gravity main, assisted by a suction pump. The baths, constructed on the south side of Scarbrough Avenue (East), opened later in the year.

SHIP 'ELIZA' brought to Skegness from Kings Lynn in May for breaking up but purchased by Joe Wingate and transformed into a marine museum featuring the skeleton of a 70 foot whale.

STEAM TRAMWAY. Plans made for a steam tramway from Skegness to link up with the Alford to Sutton-on-Sea Tramway, via Ingoldmells, and Hogsthorpe, the terminus being opposite Skegness railway station. Nothing came of it and the Alford-Sutton Tramway stopped running in 1884 after a branch railway line connected Sutton to Willoughby.

AUGUST BANK HOLIDAY brought in a record 22,000 trippers and by 6 pm.all shops and refreshment rooms had run out of food. As the visitors crowded into the station for the return journey the trains were unable to get away on the single line and thousands filled the nearby streets, the last train not moving out until 2 o'clock in the morning.

1883 PIER STEAMERS. Skegness Steamboat Company formed to run trips from the pierhead landing-stage with chartered paddle-steamers. Excursions across the Wash to Hunstanton, costing three shillings, were very popular and other steamers brought day visitors from Boston, Lynn and other ports.

FIRE ENGINE, costing £175, purchased by Parish Vestry, the Midland Counties Insurance Company contributing £50 and Lord Scarbrough £25.

ROAD MAINTENANCE. A parish meeting on July 14 considered a notice from the Earl of Scarbrough intimating his wish to dedicate as public highways, Grand Parade, South Parade, Rutland Road, Wainfleet Road and Alexander Road. The vestry resolved that only Rutland Road was 'of sufficient utility to the inhabitants ... to justify their being kept in repair at the expense of the Parish' and refused to accept responsibility. At a later meeting, Sea View Lane was dedicated a public highway, to be known as Sea View Road.

POLICE STATION, Roman Bank, built at a cost of £1,200. The building contained three cells and a courtroom and was in charge of a police inspector.

PARISH OFFICERS appointed at the annual meeting of the Parish Vestry on March 20 were: W.P. Moody and Hobson Dunkley, overseers; Charles F. Grantham and Joseph Wingate, surveyors of highways; E.Marshall, dikereeve; J.Tapster, constable; H.V.Tippet, assessor of taxes.

RECESSION. After the initial burst of building activity, work on the new town came almost to a standstill because of national depression affecting industry and agriculture and lasting into the 1890s. Large villas in Lumley Road, South Parade and Wainfleet Road remained unsold and Rutland Terrace, Rutland Road, attracting few buyers sent builder T.S.Kassell into bankruptcy. In 1884 railway excursions fell by half.

1884 ANNUAL PARISH MEETING held in the National School in April under the chairmanship of H.V.Tippet, agent for the Earl of Scarbrough. It was reported that rates collected during the year amounted to £248 and expenditure was £209. Highway surveyors C.F.Grantham and J.Wingate stated that all the roads were in good condition, but when T.Greenwood asked if a causeway could be added to High Street he was told that it was too narrow.

NINTH EARL OF SCARBROUGH, the 'father' of modern Skegness, died. Born in 1813, as a young man he became paralysed after falling from his horse and for the remainder of his life he was confined to a wheelchair. He began the building of the resort town in the late 1870s and financed most of the public services and amenities.

SKEGNESS VOLUNTEERS, numbering 37 men, used the Sea View Hotel as their drill hall, forming part of 'F' Company of the 1st. Battalion, Lincolnshire Regiment, whose headquarters were Spilsby Drill Hall.

THE SKEGNESS POLKA songsheet advertised in-the Skegness Herald of January 4 on sale for 1s.6d. (8p) at White's Music Warehouse,Lumley Road.

1885

PARISH CHEST. The Easter Vestry authorised the purchase of a new parish chest as the existing one was almost filled with the parish records. The rector stated that the oldest parish registry dated from 1500.

SKEGNESS LOCAL BOARD elected under the Local Government Act, 1884. An election was held in September when Charles Houghton topped the poll with 348 votes, one ahead of G.Dunkley and C.F.Grantham. Others elected to the first Skegness Local Board were H.V.Tippet, S.Clarke, J.Crawshaw, F.L.Wardle, C.Hildred, H.E.Iremonger, A.W.Rowley, E.Marshall and W.E.Swift in that order. There were 16 unsuccessful candidates. At the first Board meeting, Colonel Iremonger was elected chairman.

HORNCASTLE PARLIAMENTARY DIVISION (which included Skegness) established as one of seven new Lincolnshire constituencies. Prior to that date, the county had three parliamentary divisions, North, Mid and South Lincolnshire, Skegness being in Mid-Lincs. Horncastle was the only town in the new division with more than three thousand inhabitants, but Spilsby was adopted as the returning town because of its more central location. The Hon. Edward Stanhope, who had represented Mid-Lincolnshire, became the first member elected for Horncastle and he served as Secretary of State for War, 1887-92 in Lord Salisbury's administration.

SWITCHBACK near the pier entrance, North Parade, opened.in July It was located just north of the pier on ground later taken up by the Grosvenor House and Dorchester Hotels. The Switchback was a popular attraction for many years until,overshadowed by the new Figure 8 Railway at the other end of North Parade; it was demolished in 1911. In Roller Coasters (1992), Robert E.Preedy stated that the Skegness Switchback was the first to operate in this country.

1886	LIBRARY. Skegness Parish Magazine for February mentioned that St. Matthew's Church lending library had over 400 volumes available to parishioners at a charge of a halfpenny a week. The rector requested borrowers to keep the books clean~not to read them close to the fire or allow small children to damage them. The library was forced to close about a year later through lack of support, illiteracy still being very prevalent at that time.
	EASTER VESTRY. The annual meeting was attended by only about twenty members of the public, 'a very small gathering compared with previous years,' commented the rector, Rev.F.Baldwin, who presided. He went on to explain that much of the business formerly in the hands of the parish vestry had passed to the control of the recently elected Local Board.
	CRICKET. The Australian Touring XI played a match on the Cricket Ground against a Skegness & Visitor's XV the home side winning by 8 wickets. The 'Skegness' side, with its extra four, included a number of county players and was captained by Richard Daft of Notts and England. Australia scored 103 and 140 , and Skegness, 187 and 57 for 6. The game attracted nearly six thousand spectators over the three days, but it was still a financial failure. The Australians stayed at the Lumley Hotel, close to the ground.
1887	WHALE CAPTURED. On Sunday morning, April 21, a young rorqual whale was sighted off the pierhead and was shot and beached by local fishermen and others. Over the Easter holiday weekend the carcase 47 feet in length, was exhibited to thousands of visitors and subsequently auctioned by G.H.Cash and knocked down to a gentleman from Hull for thirty guineas.
1888	PUBLIC OFFICES. At the Annual Vestry Meeting on March 23, Mr.J.Crawshaw drew attention to the great inconvenience and expense, particularly for the poor, because certain offices were out of town, viz: the medical officer for the poor (Burgh), the relieving officer (Alford) and the registrar of births and deaths (Spilsby). It was agreed to make representations to the appropriate authorities for local officers to be appointed. Unfortunately, in spite of continuing efforts, it was a number of years before any improvement was effected.'
	MARINE GARDENS completed in front of the parades south of the pier. After the retaining wall was built in 1878, sand began to build uP and the Earl of Scarbrough dealt with the accretion by planting grass and shrubs to provide a more pleasing aspect from the promenade.
	FOUNTAIN. The ornamental iron fountain incorporating gas lamps in Lumley Square removed for road safety. In October, the fountain, minus the gas lamps, was re-erected in the Marine Gardens just south of the pier.

HORTICULTURAL SOCIETY established with a view to holding an annual autumn show.

CHURCH DIFFERENCES. At the annual Easter Vestry Meeting on April 6, churchwarden H.V.Tippet (the Earl of Scarbrough's Agent) resigned his office because of the form of service favoured by the rector Rev.F.Baldwin. Mr. Tippet and other influential members of St. Matthew's Church accused the rector of popish practices and they subsequently formed the St. Paul's Free Church of England, building a new place of worship in what later became Beresford Avenue. The breakaway group lasted six or seven years, but after a new rector came to Skegness they closed down and rejoined St.Matthew's congregation. Their iron church in Beresford Avenue was taken over by the local Baptists, but still known as St. Paul's.

1889   LINDSEY COUNTY COUNCIL established, with effect from April 1 (Local Government Act, 1888). Elections had been held in January and Skegness's first county councillor was Robert James Epton, farmer, of Bank House, Croft. He served as the Skegness representative until 1901 when he was appointed an alderman, continuing on the County Council until 1907.

MAGISTRATES. The 144 magistrates in the administrative county of Lindsey included 71 'squires' and 41 clergymen and 'between them, gentry and clergy dominated the bench,' (Quoted from Arthur Wickstead's history of Lindsey County Council, published 1948.)

1890   SCHOOL INSPECTION. The Diocesan School Inspector, Rev. Edwin Roberts, rector of Candlesby, examined the pupils of Skegness National School and reported that they showed a good knowledge of the Catechism and Prayer Book and did fairly well on questions relating to the Old and New Testaments. No mention was made of the 'three Rs".

COW CLUB. Skegness & District Cow Club formed at a public meeting in the Lion Hotel on March 3.

TRIPPERS' PARADISE. John Murray's 'Handbook of Lincolnshire' described Skegness as 'now one of the most crowded and popular sea-side resorts in England for day-excursionists from the midland counties, but not much to be recommended for quieter visitors. A few years ago, Skegness was a quiet little village, reached by an omnibus from Burgh Station, with two good village inns and excellent sands, well suited for children. Now it is the noisiest and most crowded of the Lincolnshire sea-side places, except Cleethorpes, invaded every day during the summer by an enormous number of excursionists.'

1891	NO HAWKERS (OR FREEBREATHERS!). In the summer that year the Earl of Scarbrough's agent posted notices prohibiting unauthorised traders operating on the beach, stating that the foreshore was Lord Scarbrough's private property. Subsequently, a letter from a London visitor appeared in a local newspaper addressed to the Earl, as follows: 'Upon paying a visit to Skegness, I find that there are notices ... advising the fact that the sands above high-water mark are private property of your lordship and your fellow-countrymen use the same on sufferance only. I write for the purpose of returning to your lordship the enclosed oyster shell. My little girl, aged five and unaware of the ideas that obtain in this country as to the sacred rights of property purloined the shell from your lordship's beach without my knowledge. I hasten to make reparation. And she, my lord, is not the only offender against your estate. I myself breathed some of your air whilst standing upon your sands, looking over your sea. It is certain that more oxygen was consumed at Skegness than if I had not been there, but I sincerely hope your lordship did not go short on that account.'
1893	SANDS SERVICES inaugurated when local Baptist, Richard Hudson, invited the Pioneer Mission to Skegness. They sent the Rev. George Goodchild to conduct the evangelical gatherings on the beach and, when the Skegness Baptist Church was formed a year later, he was appointed their first minister, a post he occupied until his death in 1905.

'SHANNON' DISASTER occurred on Saturday, July 8, when the pleasure sailing ship, 'Shannon', sank off Gibraltar Point with the loss of 28 lives, including the two boatmen, Edward and Edwin Grunnill. A sudden squall was the cause of the wreck and the vessel went down before the boatmen had time to haul in the sails. There were only three survivors, picked up by Jabez Grunnill in his small fishing boat.

ROYAL CELEBRATION, on the occasion of the marriage of the future King George V and Queen Mary, marked by a grand street procession. Three days later occurred the terrible 'Shannon' disaster recorded above. |
| 1894 | CHURCH ORGANIST at St.Matthew's Church, Miss Garner, asked for an increase of salary at the annual Vestry Meeting in March, but 'owing to depleted finances it was decided to allow her to give an organ recital and take the collection.' Sexton John Dunn also asked for a raise but said he "did not know if he could give an organ recital' and was granted an increase of £1 per annum. |

1895   SKEGNESS URBAN DISTRICT COUNCIL instituted under the new Local Government Act, 1894, the first election taking place on December 19, with the single polling station at the National School, Roman Bank. Charles Fred Grantham, chairman of the outgoing Local Board, topped the poll, the other eleven elected members, in order of votes recorded, being A.W.Rowley, S.G.Randall, J.Barlow, C.Houghton, F.Kirkby, J.Borman, J.S.Sills, G.Dunkley, W.P.Moody, C.R.Pawson and G.J.Crofts. Eight of the twelve elected had been members of the Local Board. There were 15 unsuccessful candidates.

SKEGNESS GOLF CLUB (later Seacroft G.C.) formed at a meeting in the Vine Hotel on January 31. Rules were adopted and the Earl of Scarbrough was elected president, Major C.A.Swan of Aswardby Hall, captain, and Skegness rector, Rev.C.P.Disbrowe, honorary secretary. The first tee was then in front of the hotel and the nine-hole links was officially opened on April 24 when a match was played between J.H.Taylor, the 1894 Open champion, and G.K.Wilson, the club's newly appointed professional.

FISHERIES. A fisheries report stated that at Skegness this year, fishing boats landed 220,000 crabs and 11 tons, 5 cwts. of shrimps. (Quoted by G.H.J.Dutton in his 'Ancient and Modern Skegness', (1921, p. 150.)

1896   RAILWAY. The Great Northern Railway Company purchased the whole of the Firsby to Skegness line from the local company for £76,500, as from January.

1897   CYCLE RACES held on the Richmond Drive Cricket Ground for the first time. The 2 mile handicap resulted: 1. A.G.Rowley 2. C.J.Farmer 3. A.Dunn. A cycle track round the ground provided two-and-a-half laps to the mile.

1898   FORESHORE LEASE. After five Skegness councillors had attended the London offices of the Board of Trade, the Urban District Council was granted a lease of the foreshore (technically the beach between high and low water mark) at a nominal rent of £1 per year, enabling them to remove sand and gravel at an agreed tonnage annually.

UNDERGROUND LAVATORIES in Lumley Road completed with government loan of £500. They remained a full century, until demolition in 2001, replaced by a new building in Briar Way.

ROMAN CATHOLIC CHURCH, Grosvenor Road, officially opened on September 29 by the Bishop of Nottingham. It cost £500 and seated 500 people.

FOOTBALL. At a match on the Cricket Ground, Skegness & District FC beat Boston Victoria 3-1. The referee was Frank Forman, Nottingham Forest and England full back. (March.)

CHURCH CONTROVERSY. When W.E.Gladstone died in May, Skegness rector, Rev.C.P.Disbrowe, a diehard Tory, refused to have the Dead March in Saul played at St.Matthew's Church, as ordered by the bishop of the diocese. After many protests and letters in the Skegness Herald, the Dead March, to mark the passing of the former Liberal prime minister was played after the Whit Sunday service.

ROBIN HOOD RIFLES held their annual camp at Gibraltar Point during August Bank Holiday week. The cycle section pedalled all the way from Nottingham, breakfasting in Sleaford. The volunteer regiment was formed in Nottingham in 1859 and held their first annual camp at Skegness in 1883. The Boer War began in 1899 and 1898 was the last occasion the volunteers camped at Skegness.

1899

BRYTHWEN HIGH SCHOOL established at the junction of Algitha Road and Lumley Avenue with principals, the Misses Annie and Kate Robinson. A school for young ladies, it advertised as preparing them for public examinations and its sporting activities included tennis, hockey, swimming, cycling and croquet. In 1922 it became a preparatory school for both boys and girls, known as Lyndhurst College, but closed in the 1930s.

The building was later purchased by Nottingham Co-operative Society to be converted to the Lyndhurst Social Club for their local staff, members and friends. The Co-op. placed the building on the market in 2000, but the club has continued under the same name since then under private ownership.

PRIMITIVE METHODISTS vacated their chapel on the west side of Roman Bank to move across the road to a new building, costing £2,070. It was formally opened on April 13. The old chapel was sold for £150 and converted, to three dwelling houses. (A Church Parlour was added at the rear in 1924, when an exterior wall tablet was unveiled in memory of nine members of the congregation who had sacrificed their lives in the 1914 -18 war.)

WESLEY MANSE,15 Lumley Avenue, built for occupation by the minister of the Wesleyan Methodist Chapel, Algitha Road. (It was sold in 1931 and in 1935 the minister was rehoused in a new, and smaller residence in Ida Road. The building is now a solicitor s office

CLOCK TOWER, commemorating Queen Victoria's Diamond Jubilee (1897) officially opened on August 11 by the Countess of Scarbrough. The construction was funded by public donations.

HILDREDS HOTEL reopened (after purchase by Bass & Co. two years earlier) on completion of extensive alterations and refurbishment. Manager F.F.Mead was a former captain of Northampton Rugby Club and a well-known amateur boxer.

1899   FIRST SKEGNESS MOTOR CAR arrived in the town on January 26. The Daimler had been purchased by a syndicate of local businessmen composed of Bill Berry, garage owner, Freddy Kirkby, landlord of the Lion Hotel, Joe Wingate who owned the Whale Museum and Richard Lloyd. With a hired chauffeur, they collected the car in London, the epic journey to Skegness taking 3½ days, with numerous stops for 'refuelling' (car and crew) at pubs along the Great North Road. Top Speed was 12 miles an hour. The vehicle was purchased to provide short rides for visitors as motor cars were quite a novelty at that date.

FOOTBALL. The Willoughby Cup Competition initiated for football clubs in the Horncastle Parliamentary Division by Lord Willoughby de Eresby, MP. The oldest football competition in East Lindsey, the original members were Alford Apprentices, Alford United, Horncastle Town, Horncastle Wednesday, Skegness & District, Spilsby Rangers, Stickney and Woodhall Spa. The first season was made difficult because of many players volunteering for service in the Boer War.

AUGUST BANK HOLIDAY. The railway brought in 19,250 day trippers.

THE BATTLE OF FLOWERS was again a feature of the annual carnival and the Skegness Herald reported that the floral fight on Grand Parade found the fair sex putting to flight their male opponents.

COUNCIL FINANCES. The annual statement showed that loan debt stood at £1,464. Road repairs had cost £426, street lighting £183, sewage disposal £657 and house refuse removal £167. The refuse collectors had received a wage increase of a shilling to bring their weekly pay packet to sixteen shillings (80p) for a 47 hour week.

1900   GREAT NORTHERN RAILWAY converted the single line between Firsby Junction and Skegness to a double track, roofed the station with glass and carried out other improvements. Cow Bank and Croft Bank stations were renamed Seacroft and Havenhouse respectively.

THE PARK established along two ridges of sand dunes between Scarbrough Avenue and the Sea View Hotel. The Earl of Scarbrough had intended selling it off as building plots, but as development slumped in the 1890s recession he decided to leave it as open parkland. It remained largely in a wild state and eventually became known as the Jungle.

FRED CLEMENTS brought his first concert party to Skegness, performing from a small wooden stage on the sands.

BOYS' BRIGADE, known as the 1st. Skegness Company, formed under Capt.C.F.Grantham, supported by Lieutenants R.Batley and G.C.Dunkley.

RABBIT COURSING held in a field near the Ship Hotel, Burgh Road.

LICENCES granted by Skegness Council included 89 Hackney Carriages, 92 horses, mules and asses, 17 pleasure boats, 35 four-wheeled barrows, 287 two-wheeled barrows, 59 pitches for stalls and rides, 115 hawkers' baskets and 10 sand bridges over the creeks. Total income from licences amounted to £122.18s.11d. The year's takings from the Lumley Road underground lavatories was £164.0s.7d.

GENERAL ELECTION In the October election, Lord Willoughby de Eresby (Conservative) was returned as member for the Horncastle Division, although with a reduced majority of thirteen hundred over his Liberal challenger.

DRUGS DEATH. A sixty year old Winthorpe woman died from laudanum poisoning, but it was stated at the inquest that the taking of laudanum and opium, especially by women, had now decreased. Formerly, laudanum was frequently administered to babies to keep them quiet.

1901 TELEPHONES. Skegness connected to the public telephone service, the exchange at the Post Office opening with 26 local subscribers.

CORONATION WALK opened to commemorate the crowning of Edward VII.

SKEGNESS CHORAL SOCIETY formed with Wainfleet schoolmaster Alfred Rogerson as choirmaster.

FOOTBALL. Skegness & District FC. beat Alford 1 - 0 in final of the Willoughby Cup, played at Spilsby.

1902 SKEGNESS OLD FOLKS' TREAT inaugurated on initiative of G.H.J. Crofts, with a tea and concert in the Pleasure Gardens Pavilion. It became an annual event until it ceased in 1926, a few years after Mr. Crofts' death.

D.H.LAWRENCE, famous novelist and poet, and author of Lady Chatterley's Lover, as a youth recovering from pneumonia, spent several weeks at his aunt's guest house on South Parade.

BANK ROBBERY. The manager of the Skegness branch of the Capital & Counties Bank convicted of embezzlement and jailed for five years.

SMUGGLING MURDER. When extensive alterations were being carried out at the Vine Hotel, a skeleton was found immured in the brickwork, together with brass buttons bearing the royal insignia. It was believed to be the remains of a local customs officer who had disappeared in mysterious circumstances nearly a hundred years before. He had probably interrupted a smuggling operation and been quietly silenced and hidden in a building where such activities were frequently planned.

1903 ST. MATTHEW'S CHURCH. A thanksgiving service on July 22, conducted by the Bishop of Lincoln, to mark completion of the church. Ground subsidence had caused long delays as well as dismantling the partly built tower, although the foundation stone had been laid in 1879.

PASSIVE RESISTANCE. In protest against the Balfour Education Act, eighteen Skegness residents who had refused to pay the portion of the rates allocated for educational purposes, were summoned to Spilsby police court. All nonconformists, they claimed it was a sectarian tax, but were found guilty and their goods distrained for payment.

HIGH TIDE in November flooded the Marine Gardens and reached up to the clock tower, said to be the highest tide since 1897.

RAILWAY COMPLAINT. A public meeting, chaired by John Canning, protested about the inadequate railway service between Skegness and Lincoln, which was via Boston. The Great Northern Railway could promise no quicker route and it was resolved to invite the rival Midland Railway to lay a direct line between the two places. Negotiations were subsequently begun, but nothing came of it, but ten years later, the GNR built fifteen miles of new line to link Kirkstead, near Woodhall Spa, with the East Lincolnshire Railway at Bellwater Junction, just south of Firsby. The new route did not come into operation until 1 June 1913, but it did eventually avoid the long detour to Boston and saved a lot of travelling time.

1904 THE STONE LION, which had stood on the roof of the Lion Hotel since its opening in 1881, was brought down to pavement level on Roman Bank, because it was considered dangerous. There it remained for more than ninety years providing immense pleasure to generations of small children who delighted to be given 'a ride' on its broad, hard back.

CYCLE RACES held on the cricket ground at a sports meeting organised by Skegness & District Social Cycling Club.

TRAIN TRIPS. Skegness Council protested to the Great Northern Railway about the noisy and drunken day trippers upsetting the staying visitors and getting the town a bad name. The railway company declined responsibility, stating that they were the servants of the public and were obliged to convey people wherever they wanted to go, at times convenient to them.

1905 POST OFFICE moved from shop premises in Lumley Road to a new GPO on the corner of Roman Bank and Algitha Road with a full time staff and postmistress Mrs. Elizabeth Cutler. (The building is now LLoyds-T.S.B. Bank.)

	MOTOR RACES held on sands for the first time, promoted by Nottingham Automobile Club.
1906	SEWERAGE. Cowbank sewage sisposal works, south of Richmond Drive, extended to cope with the rising population.
1907	FIRST TAXI licensed in Skegness, a Darracq car owned by George Scott.
	FIRST SKEGNESS JP. Charles Frederick Grantham of The Hall, Roman Bank, appointed to serve at Spilsby Petty Sessions.
	AVENUE CLUB established as 'a gentlemen's club' with premises in Lumley Avenue. For a number of years they occupied the building next door to the former Midland Bank, now HSBC, but moved across the road some years later. Still located there, the building was formerly the residence and surgery of Dr. Stanley Wallace, general practitioner and part-time Medical Officer of Health to the Skegness UD Council. The Avenue Club celebrates its centenary in 2007.
1908	POLICE COURT. After repeated applications, Petty Sessions held in Skegness for the first time - May to October only - saving the long journey to Spilsby. The courts were held in the Council Offices and the National School on Roman Bank.
	COUNTY INFANTS' SCHOOL, Cavendish Road, opened, transferring pupils from the former Assembly Rooms in High Street, which had been used as a temporary school for infants.
	FIGURE 8 SWITCHBACK RAILWAY opened at North Parade.
	JOLLY FISHERMAN POSTER, drawn by John Hassall, first released for Easter to advertise half-day train trips from King's Cross to Skegness for three shillings return.
	BATTLE OF GRANNY'S OPENING took place when Lawrence Kirk, owner of the North Shore Golf Links, in course of construction, blocked up a footpath leading from Roman Bank to the seashore. Winthorpe residents, led by Cllr. Samuel Moody, tore down the barricades and Kirk prosecuted them for trespass and wilful damage. The case came before the magistrates at Spilsby Session House in May, when the defendants were found not guilty'. The right of way was confirmed and the footpath ordered to be reinstated and it is still used by the public.

OLD AGE PENSION first instituted, with payment of 5s. (25p) for single people over 70 years of age and 7s.6d. (38p) for married couples, providing their annual income was less than £39. It was estimated that this allowance saved more than five million elderly people from the workhouse. Not until 1925 was the pension increased to ten shillings (50p) for everybody over 65 years of age.

1909   SKEGNESS CO-OP formed as Skegness & District Co-operative Society with a grocery and butcher shop in High Street and deliveries by horse and van to Wainfleet and other nearby places.

1910   WATERWORKS. Skegness Urban District Council purchased the water undertaking from the Earl of Scarbrough for £42,000, resulting in reduced charges for the consumers. A piped supply from underground reservoirs at Welton-le-Marsh had been laid five years earlier.

NORTH SHORE GOLF LINKS officially opened with a match between British Open winners, Harry Vardon, James Braid, J.H.Taylor and George Duncan.

PIER STEAMERS ceased operating from the pierhead, partly because of sandbanks building up in the Wash, but mainly owing to the landing-stage becoming unsafe.

BOYS' BRIGADE. 2nd. Skegness Company formed in February under Capt. Robert Batley, with Adjutant C.H.Major and Lieutenants R.Barnett, J.S.Kinsley, C.Barney and A.E.Fletcher.

BOY SCOUTS. Scoutmaster Tom Wiles resigned and was replaced by Scoutmaster W. Repton.

1911   LAWN THEATRE, Lumley Road, opened by Fred Clements on site of his open-air concerts on the lawn next to the Bass-owned Hildreds Hotel.

ARCADIA THEATRE, Drummond Road, built for Fred Clements

SANDS PAVILION erected on the south side of Lumley Pullover (Tower Esplanade) for refreshments and dancing. It became the Cafe Dansant after the Great War and later still, the Foreshore Centre before its demolition in 1971.

CENTRAL HALL, Roman Bank, built by John Henry Canning for public meetings, concerts, dances and other occasions. (It was later a cinema and is now a bingo hall.)

ST. PAUL'S BAPTIST CHURCH opened on Good Friday, April 14, replacing a corrugated iron building nearby which became the school hall. The new church cost £2,740.

SWITCHBACK, near the pier, dismantled. It had stood since 1885, but suffered in competition with the newer Figure 8 at the opposite end of North Parade.

FIRST MOTOR PLEASURE BOAT began operating at Skegness, owned by W.Jefferies. The Monaco was powered by a Daimler engine and could do ten knots and carry ten passengers.

BOYS' CAMP. Wigan Church Lads' Brigade camped in Richmond Drive during August Bank Holiday week when 2,600 boys and officers were accommodated in more than 300 tents.

CAPITAL & COUNTIES BANK moved from Estate Offices to Lumley Road, becoming Lloyds Bank in 1918.

MUSEUM SHIP, Eliza, blown over on a spring tide and, soon afterwards, the hulk and its contents were auctioned off on the sands by George Dunkley. The ship was knocked down to Mr.W.Parish of Hogsthorpe for £16.10s.

1912   LINCOLNSHIRE AGRICULTURAL SHOW held in Skegness for the first time, located in a field in Richmond Drive. A day or two before opening a foot-and-mouth outbreak brought about a nationwide stand-still order and cattle already on the way were turned back. The show opened, but with no livestock, yet attendance over the two days was still 17,333.

SKEGNESS LIFEBOAT carried out one of its most notable rescues when, on November 13, in very heavy seas, it went to the aid of the Norwegian cargo ship, Azha, stranded on the Skegness Middle Sands. The Samuel Lewis took off the eight man crew and, subsequently, coxswain Matthew Grunnill and second-cox Montague Grunnill were awarded silver medals by the King of Norway.

1913   SKEGNESS COTTAGE HOSPITAL officially opened on May 19 by the Countess of Scarbrough, commemorating the coronation of George V in 1911. The money was raised with donations, bazaars, etc., and the building site in Dorothy Avenue was given by the Earl of Scarbrough.

RAILWAY from Lincoln to Skegness, via Kirkstead and Little Steeping opened on June 1 by the Great Northern Railway Company.

SKEGNESS SALVATION ARMY CORPS formed on May 22 at a meeting in a High Street cafe.

BOYS' BRIGADE CAMP at Spilsby in May attended by 2nd. and 3rd. Skegness Companies, totalling 66 boys, under Captains C.H.Major and R.Batley respectively.

FIRST AIR DISPLAY at Skegness in June when pioneer aviator, B.C.Hucks, during a tour of Lincolnshire, gave flying demonstrations and flights in his 70 h.p. Bleriot monoplane from a field in Richmond Drive. Hucks was a test pilot in the Great War and died in the disastrous influenza epidemic of 1919.

LICENCING. Skegness Urban District Council granted licences for 94 Hackney carriages, 62 horses, mules and asses, 19 pleasure boats, 32 bathing vans 141 barrows and 189 hawkers' baskets.

SEA VIEW HOTEL added an extension with roof garden fronting on North Parade.

ROADWORKS. In his annual report, the Council surveyor stated that Seacroft Esplanade was under construction and Wilford Grove and several other streets in Seacroft had been surfaced and paved. Roman Bank had been kerbed and paved as far as Burgh Road junction.

1914   WINTHORPE VICARAGE disunited from Burgh-le-Marsh on March 19.

SKEGNESS & DISTRICT PIG CLUB held its 43rd. annual dinner, having been formed in 1871.

AUGUST BANK HOLIDAY saw the town filled with visitors as the excursion trains followed one another in quick succession. War with Germany was declared the following day and on the Wednesday morning the local contingent of Territorials entrained to report for duty. The Territorials were a voluntary part-time Army reserve.

NAVAL CAPTURE. The German schooner, Gerhard, intercepted by two gunboats five miles off the pierhead and escorted to Boston.

LOVAT SCOUTS, a Scottish mounted regiment, after quartering in Grimsby, rode into Skegness in late December with 3,000 horses, Brigadier General Lord Lovat arriving next day. Lord Lovat's second-in-command was Major Ian Bullough whose wife was Lily Elsie, the famous musical comedy star who spent some time in Skegness with her husband. Lord Lovat's wife and young son also lived in the town whilst the Scots were here and in the Second World War the son led the commando raid on Boulogne. A later Lord Lovat, in 1998 became the youngest peer to take a seat in the House of Lords, aged twenty-one.

1915   PARISH HALL, Ida Road, officially opened on June 15 by Mrs L.Martin-Simpson who had contributed £500 of the total cost of £700 towards its building. Some years later it was renamed the Church Hall after considerable controversy.

GASWORKS. Skegness Council purchased the gas undertaking from the Skegness Gas Company.

JOY WHEEL, near the Figure 8 Switchback, destroyed by fire. The crackling of flames in the early hours was mistaken in some quarters for rifle fire, giving rise to rumours that the Germans had landed!

JOHN D.PLAYER, cigarette manufacturer of Alexandra Park, Nottingham, sued Skegness butcher, Herbert Manton, for damage to his motor car amounting to £9.10s. The Rolls-Royce was parked in Drummond Road when Manton's horse and cart backed into it. Spilsby magistrates found defendant guilty of dangerous driving, with damages and costs for Mr. Player.

1918   VOTES FOR WOMEN. Women over the age of thirty were permitted to vote for the first time, following a long and desperately brave campaign by the Suffragettes. The voting age was reduced to twenty-one, the same as a man, in 1929.

1919   FIRST LADY COUNCILLOR elected to Skegness Urban District Council in the person of Miss M. E. Rankin. Mary Rankin started a toy factory manufacturing Jolly Fisherman dolls, held dancing classes and became the first manageress of the Sun Castle when it opened in 1933.

SHIP THROUGH PIER. On the 8 o'clock morning tide of March 21, the Amsterdam schooner, Europa, 9,200 tons, dragging her anchor and out of control, plunged into the middle of the pier. Anchored opposite the Sea View Hotel overnight, the skipper had ignored warnings from lifeboat coxswain Matt Grunnill to put out more anchors or move his position and the lifeboatmen stood ready next morning to give aid. After being extricated from the pier, the badly damaged vessel was towed to Grimsby by tug. The large gap in the pier was linked by a 'temporary' bridge which remained for twenty years until a matching reconstruction was completed in February 1939. The work was carried out by Chris Gutteridge, structural engineer, Burgh le Marsh.

1920   COUNCIL OFFICES. The Earl of Scarbrough's Estate Offices, Roman Bank, at the corner of Algitha Road, purchased by Skegness U.D. Council. The earl removed his offices to 29, Algitha Road, previously occupied by the Council.

CAFE DANSANT became the new title of the Sands Pavilion on Tower Esplanade, advertising 'light luncheons and dainty afternoon teas and an American Fountain for iced fruit drinks.' Evening dances and 'tea dances' were held in the summer months, whilst various functions took place during the winter, including Miss Rankin's children's dancing classes on Saturdays.

YMCA HOLIDAY CAMP, Grosvenor Road, became Skegness's first holiday camp. Established with surplus army tents and other equipment by the Nottingham branch of the Young Men's Christian Association, it was initially restricted to ex-servicemen.

MIDLAND BANK opened in Lumley Road on the west corner of Lumley Avenue, after demolition of Frith's Restaurant.

POLICE BRAVERY rewarded by presentation of the Police Medal to Superintendent Joseph Hutchinson, Sergeant Cross and Constable Rodwell for capturing two armed robbers for whom a countrywide search was being made. The policemen cornered Topley and Ridley in a car at Thrall's Garage - now Morrison filling station - and disarmed them after a violent struggle.

1921 FORESHORE DEVELOPMENT SCHEME presented to Skegness Council in December. Prepared by town surveyor, Rowland H.Jenkins, the plan included the reconstruction of Tower Pullover (Tower Esplanade) and provision of tennis courts, a putting green, bowling greens, boating lake, gardens and a children's playground. The scheme was approved and it was agreed to apply for government loan of £1,250, subject to negotiations with the Earl of Scarbrough for purchase of the foreshore being satisfactorily concluded.

TOWER THEATRE, Lumley Road, opened by Fred Clements on July 25, after he terminated his tenancy of the Lawn Theatre. Like many early 'movie cinemas' it was officially termed a theatre, even after cinemas were eventually distinguished from live-show theatres. The first feature film on the opening night at the Tower was 'Carnival.' starring Matheson Lang.

LAWN THEATRE taken over by Henri DeMond who ran it as a cinema until its closure in 1934.

1922 LINCOLNSHIRE AGRICULTURAL SHOW held in Skegness for the second time, on July 19. The location was again in Richmond Drive and the attendance 22,598.

SKEGNESS STANDARD launched on July 5, by the Boston owned Lincolnshire Standard, with Arthur E. Fletcher editor.

THE CASINO, North Parade opened on June 1 as a ballroom and restaurant. The site had previously been occupied by the Alhambra open air roller skating rink and is now a bingo hall known as the North Parade Social Club.

1922 FORESHORE PURCHASE completed by Skegness U.D.Council from the Earl of Scarbrough, the document being sealed at a Council Meeting on January 14. It included the foreshore, parades and Marine Gardens from the Seacroft Hotel to the Figure 8 Railway, North Parade, taking in the Pleasure Gardens and Pavilion and the Cafe Dansant, but excluding the pier. The total cost was £15,750 and, omitting legal charges was made up as follows:

	£
Pleasure Gardens, including Pavilion.	8,600
Marine Gardens and Seashore.	3,500
The Sands Pavilion.	3,000
	15,100

It will be noted that the actual seashore cost only £3.500, a generous arrangement by the earl, but much undervalued compared with the other two items.

TOWN BUS SERVICE launched by William T.Berry who was Skegness's first garage owner. The service was augmented with a charabanc to Boston market every Wednesday. A few months later, the Stinson brothers formed Skegness Motor Service Company

FLOODING. In October the sea broke through at Ingoldmells, near Mastin's Corner, flooding 103 acres and reaching up to Roman Bank.

FIRST SKEGNESS COUNCIL HOUSES completed by five local building contractors, Joseph Crawshaw, William Greetham, Holmes and Sons, Henry Lill and Frederick W.Walker, the total cost for the 99 houses amounting to £87,674, which was very expensive at that time.

NORTH PARADE, a gravel road, reconstructed with a tarmac surface and footpaths.

GENERAL BRAMWELL BOOTH, son of the founder of the Salvation Army, visited Skegness, attending a crowded gathering in the Baptist Church.

SKEGNESS AMATEUR OPERATIC SOCIETY formed and presented Gilbert and Sullivan's HMS Pinafore, with proceeds going to Skegness Cottage Hospital.

1923   TOWER ESPLANADE, the former Lumley or Clock Tower Pullover, opened as a tarmac road with wide pavements, the first stage of the Council's foreshore development scheme. Known locally as 'Jenkins' Pier', after the town surveyor, many believed it would be washed down by the first spring tide and there was some 'I told you so' glee when tidal damage occurred during the early stages of construction to confirm the pessimistic forecasts

BOATING LAKE, a major item on the foreshore plan, approved only by the Council chairman's casting vote, many believing it would soon fill up with blown sand and others objecting to the large expenditure involved. Work was put in hand immediately and the lake, as far as the bridge, was officially opened by the Mayor of Lincoln the following Whitsun, 1924.

PLEASURELAND amusement park, North Parade, opened on the north side of the Figure 8 Switchback Railway.

MOTOR RACES on the sands revived after seventeen years, the last being held in 1906. The race meeting was held over two days on the Seacroft foreshore.

WAR MEMORIAL, outside St. Matthew's Church, unveiled by the Earl of Yarborough, Lord Lieutenant of Lincolnshire, on November 23.

HORSE RACES held on the sands, after a lapse of 34 years, attracting about four thousand spectators.

CATTLE MARKET, Albert Road, owned and operated by auctioneer George F.Ball, opened on December 4.

SKEGNESS-HORNCASTLE WALKING RACE revived, the previous occasion being in 1906. There were 37 competitors, the winner being Sid Stone who covered the 21 miles in 3 hrs. 50 mins. Quite a number of competitors turned out in the shirt and shorts they wore playing for their local football club.

GREAT NORTHERN RAILWAY became the London & North-Eastern Railway under a national railway reorganisation.

JOLLY FISHERMAN POSTER. The LNER advertising manager informed Skegness Council that the poster was 'played out' and should be replaced by a new design, but the local authority refused to consider any change.

SKEGNESS STEAM LAUNDRY, Roman Bank, taken over by Cedric Fry who modernised and extended it and eventually renamed the company Fenland Laundries. The family still control the business which has extended into other towns in the county.

AIR FLIGHTS from the Old Showground Field, Richmond Drive, operated by Capt. W.A.Rollinson with his DeHaviland biplane.

ACCIDENT BLACK SPOT. At Epton's Corner, the former notorious 'S' bend between Skegness and Wainfleet, seven accidents including one fatal, recorded on August Bank Holiday. Another driver was killed at the same spot a week later. The corner took its name from the Eptons of nearby Bank Farm in Croft parish.

SCORCHERS! Two local schoolboys, named Barnsdale and Watson, were jointly charged with driving motor-cycles to the danger of the public in Winthorpe Church Lane. Both admitted travelling at 25 mph and were fined £1 each.

STORM of some magnitude in early November, in which the lifeboat was called out, recalled a much worse occasion exactly one hundred years to the day earlier. In 1823, about sixty ships were sunk or stranded on the Lincolnshire coast, three years before the first lifeboat stations were established.

1924   MOTOR RACES held on the sands for the second successive summer. The star competitors were Malcolm Campbell and his record-breaking Bluebird, and J.C.Parry-Thomas with the 40 hp Leyland-Thomas. The track was again on the Seacroft foreshore.

CRICKET. Lincolnshire entertained Staffordshire on the Richmond Drive ground when former England bowler, Sid Barnes, took seven Lincolnshire wickets in their second innings. Lincolnshire, beaten by 112 runs, contained three Skegness players, Raymond Frearson and John and Henry Searby.

WAGES of general labourers employed by Skegness Council on their foreshore development scheme increased by 2¾d. (1p) to 11d. per hour (less than 5p) with a 47 hour week bringing in £2.15s (£2.75) less insurance contributions.

MOTOR CYCLE RACES held on the south beach in early September, attracting five thousand spectators.

TERRIERS. Three thousand Yorkshire Territorials camped in a field on Wainfleet Road during August Bank Holiday week, arriving in ten special trains from Sheffield, Leeds, Bradford and other cities and towns.

ST. JOHN'S AMBULANCE, Skegness Corps, formed.

HOCKEY. Henry Searby of Skegness Hockey Club became the first Lincolnshire player to turn out for England, in a match against France on April 4.

PUNISHMENT. At Skegness Children's Court, a local errand boy was convicted of stealing a wallet containing 4s.6d. (23p) and was sentenced to receive six strokes of the birch and fined 10s. (50p) with 17s.6d. (88p) costs. He had been bound over for a similar offence a month earlier.

TOWER ROW shops built in Lumley Road between Rutland Road and the Tower Gardens entrance, formerly part of Tower Gardens. Two of the largest occupiers were Lowndes' Arcade and Mrs. Watson's Tower Cafe and Dance Hall.

1926 WINTHORPE INCORPORATION. The parish of Winthorpe incorporated in Skegness as from April 1.'under the Lindsey (Skegness Urban District) Order, 1925. It practically doubled the area of Skegness, but with minor effect on the population, the 1921 census showing only 698 residents of Winthorpe. Bounded on the east by Roman Bank, Winthorpe did not have a sea frontage. A small area was incorporated in Addlethorpe.

CAR PARKING. Skegness's first Council car park opened in the Marine Gardens on the south side of the pier, known as the Central Car Park

C.B.FRY, famous athlete, visited Skegness by invitation of the local Liberals, with a view to being adopted as their candidate for the Horncastle constituency, but nothing came of it. Charles Burgess Fry (1872-1956) played for England at both football and cricket, as well as breaking the world record in the long jump.

LIFEBOAT TRACTOR. A caterpillar motor tractor was brought into service, replacing the team of horses used up to that date to launch and land the lifeboat.

SKEGNESS TOWN BAND reformed after disbanding at the outbreak of the First World War. Under Bandmaster Wilfred Keyworth the band made its debut on Armistice Day at the service by the war memorial. The earlier band had been formed about 1908.

BILLY BUTLIN arrived in Skegness early in the year and opened his first amusement park in the North Parade 'Jungle' area.

1927 WATER TOWER at Burgh Road Waterworks completed, but on being filled with water it started to settle, tilting alarmingly, so that it had to be hurredly emptied. Expensive steel piling was found necessary to stabilise the structure and it did not come into use until 1930. The tower was built to store water for peak periods during the summer as the pipeline could not convey water quickly enough and the tower was cheaper than laying a new large diameter main from Welton-le-Marsh.

NDFS MEMORIAL CONVALESCENT HOME, North Parade, officially opened on May 28 by HRH Princess Marie Louise as a memorial to nearly ten thousand members of the National Deposit Friendly Society who died in the Great War. Minister of Health Neville Chamberlain attended the ceremony. (The building became the Town Hall in 1964).

BEAM WIRELESS STATION, Church Lane, began operating with eight steel masts about 300 ft. high, receiving messages from India and Australia. With the transmitting station at Tetney, near Grimsby, the two stations provided the first radio connection between the two countries and Britain.

THE CO-OP STORES. Skegness Co-operative Wholesale Society amalgamated with Nottingham Co-op. The Skegness society's grocery shop at that time was at 40, High Street.

BOYS' BRIGADE. 1st. Skegness Company formed at the Baptist Church Hall on February 27 under Captain Rowland Jenkins, a prominent member of the church.

IRON FOUNTAIN moved from the Marine Gardens to what was to become the Fairy Dell. The move was necessary because of the re-development of the Marine Gardens on Grand Parade.

BUFFALOES. The Royal and Antediluvian Order of Buffaloes opened their clubhouse in Briar Way in December. (It afterwards became the Skegness Working Men's Club.) .

INDOOR BATHS, Scarbrough Avenue, purchased by EliJah Parker. In 1900, when mixed bathing was legalised, the ladies' bath had been boarded over and converted to the King's Theatre and the former men's bath was then used by both sexes.

1928   COUNCIL OFFICES DESTROYED by fire in early hours of January 11. The Roman Bank building had to be vacated and temporary accommodation was found in two pairs of newly built houses in Ida Road, whilst council meetings were held in the Church Hall just across the road. The cause of the fire was never established

NOTTINGHAMSHIRE POOR BOYS' HOLIDAY HOME officially opened by the Marchioness of Titchfield on May 30. First established as a tented camp on the Seacroft dunes in 1889, the new building in Roseberry Avenue, erected by,Skegness building contractor, William Greetham, cost about £5,000. The home was maintained by a voluntary organisation with Councillor R H Swain of Nottingham the energetic secretary. It was later taken over by Nottinghamshire County Council Education Department and renamed Roseberry House. The holiday home closed in 1993 and is now being used by Lincolnshire County Council for other purposes.

1928   OPEN-AIR BATHING POOL opened on Whit Monday, May 30, when nearly six thousand visitors passed through the turnstiles. Attendance for the season was nearly 300,000 and two successful water galas were held.

BOOTS CHEMISTS opened at 62-64, Lumley Road, about this time.

SKEGNESS SWIMMING CLUB formed June 25.

DERBYSHIRE MINERS' CONVALESCENT HOME, Winthorpe Avenue, officially opened.

WINTHORPE WAR MEMORIAL. The ancient churchyard cross close to Winthorpe church restored and dedicated as a memorial to Winthorpe men who gave their lives in the Great War.

WOOLWORTHS' 'nothing over sixpence' stores opened in Lumley Road.

SUNDAY TRADING. Skegness UD Council decided to open the boating lake and bathing pool seven days a week after a town referendum in January voted in favour.

NORTH PARADE AMUSEMENTS, between the pier and the Figure 8 Switchback, all cleared awayat the end of the season because of the erection of the National Deposit Friendly Society's Convalescent Home. A covenant covering the Jungle area declared that when permanent development commenced on either side of the parade, all temporary buildings must be removed.

PLEASURELAND amusement park, on the north side of the Figure 8 Switchback, North Parade, also removed.

1929   BUTLIN'S CENTRAL AMUSEMENT PARK, on the south side of the pier, opened at Easter, accommodating all the displaced operators from North Parade. The park was constructed by Butlin and operated by him on a twenty years' lease from the Skegness Council. He was also given permission to open on Sundays, subject to an annual rent increase of £300.

CLEMENTS' ROYAL ENTERTAINERS closed down at the end of the summer because of the covenant covering North Parade development. Fred Clements continued with his shows in the Arcadia Theatre for several years afterwards.

EMBASSY BALLROOM and Orchestral Piazza opened on Grand Parade by Skegness Urban District Council. The ballroom was reached by a central entrance from the parade (although later altered) with a restaurant below. A ramp on either side gave access to the open-air Bathing Pool. The so-called 'piazza' (Italian for a public square or open space) intervened between the Embassy building and the swimming pool, separated by a domed bandstand for use at concerts. Unfortunately, the bandstand was seldom used because of poor acoustics. The open-air piazza, bordered by colonnades formed by the overhead ramps, was used, over the years, for all sorts of activities, from dancing displays and dog shows to stabling the camels that gave rides on the beach in the early 1980s.

SIR ALAN COBHAM, record-breaking airman, gave free flights to local children in his ten-seater air-liner, Youth of Britain, part of a countrywide tour to advertise the new mode of fast travel.

CHANNEL SWIMMER, Miss Mercedes Gleitze, came to Skegness to swim the Wash to Hunstanton, but after several unsuccessful attempts from Skegness, she finally made the shorter crossing from Butterwick to Heacham in 13 hrs. 17 mins.

SALVATION ARMY CITADEL, High Street, opened on March 9.

SEACROFT SANDHILLS. Skegness UD Council acquired sandhills fronting Seacroft Esplanade and about a mile beyond to the town boundary.

VINE HOTEL, Seacroft, Skegness' oldest hotel purchased by Bateman's Brewery, Wainfleet.

COUNTY LIBRARY established a branch at the Labour Exchange in High Street, open two evenings a week and staffed by volunteers supplied by the local Toc H branch, supervised by Skegness National School headmaster, Harry Bamber.

GENERAL POST OFFICE moved to a new building on the west side of Roman Bank, just across the road from the old GPO, in early December. The new headquarters included a telephone exchange and mail sorting office.

1930 LINCOLNSHIRE AGRICULTURAL SHOW held at Skegness for the third and last time. The showground was again in Richmond Drive and the area is now incorporated in the Richmond Leisure Centre. (No attendance figures of the 1930 Show published.)

FORESHORE DEVELOPMENT. New attractions completed by the Council included the Quadrangle Gardens (later named Compass Gardens) and model yacht pond. The boating lake was extended from the bridge to Princes Parade and the Fairy Dell and Axenstrasse constructed.

SCARBROUGH AVENUE, a gravel road, was last of the town centre streets to be made up with tarmac carriageway and concrete kerbs and paving.

COURTHOUSE. Skegness's first purpose-built courthouse opened at the junction of Roman Bank and Ida Road, adjoining the police station.

GROSVENOR HOUSE HOTEL and Imperial Cafe, at the junction of North Parade and Scarbrough Avenue, built and operated by Skegness builder, Frederick W.Walker.

ROYAL NATIONAL INSTITUTION FOR THE DEAF, (RNID), Skegness branch, formed on 21 June.

1931　　　TOWN HALL. The former Council Offices on Roman Bank reopened in September after almost a complete rebuilding following the disastrous fire in 1928. The Council had debated the question of total demolition and building on a new site, but in the end had opted for rebuilding the burnt out shell.

WATERWAY opened in May, reaching from near the Figure 8 Switchback as far as the pier, with motorboat trips in both directions.

GRAF ZEPPELIN sighted over Skegness in late August, flying at 150-200 feet.

SUMMER STORM. A freak squall about 4 pm on Sunday, July 12, flooded shops in Lumley Road as well as the underground lavatories. After the rain stopped, people clustered on the crown of the road, the only dry spot, holding up the traffic.

CRICKET. A Notts county eleven played Skegness on the Cricket Ground in September, the visitors including England players, Harold Larwood, Bill Voce and George Gunn. Skegness batsman Raymond Frearson, scored 100 not out, the match ending with Skegness 138 for 3 wickets and the visitors, 210 for 6 which was declared a draw.

HOCKEY. Skegness men's hockey team completed their fifth season (1926-31) without defeat. Almost half the team played for the county and Skegness captain, John Searby, turned out for Lincolnshire in 105 consecutive matches, 130 altogether. His brother, Henry, played more than a hundred county games and four times for England. The Searby brothers and Raymond Frearson were county stalwarts at both hockey and cricket for many seasons in the 1920s and early 30s', Frearson also representing the county at golf and tennis.

TENNIS. The annual foreshore tennis tournament attracted about a hundred competitors.

GERMAN GUN, a heavy piece of artillery placed in Lumley Square after the end of the Great War, later dumped in Warth Lane, finally removed and sold to Sid Dennis as scrap iron. The cannon stood in Lumley Square for only a short time until adverse comment forced the Council to cart it off to the town outskirts where it rusted for a number of years until it was decided to scrap it.

COUNTY LIBRARY moved from High Street to the new Town Hall, still operating two evenings each week and staffed by volunteers from Toc H.

1932   MAINS ELECTRICITY. A public electricity supply, provided by Mid-Lincolnshire Electric Supply Co. Ltd., was switched on on April 23.

ILLUMINATIONS inaugurated, following the availability of mains electricity, restricted mainly to Lumley Road and the boating lake and forming part of the September carnival.

GASWORKS brought into use a large new gasholder with one million cubic feet capacity.

SUNDAY TRADING. In May, Skegness Council decided to open all their foreshore amenities on Sundays during the summer season. The boating lake and bathing pool had already been running on Sundays since 1928.

WINTER GARDENS, North Parade, opened in May as a roller skating rink, with dancing in the largest ballroom in the town. It was owned by Louis J.Henshall of the nearby Sea View Hotel, Roller skating was enjoying a boom at that date.

AIR PAGEANT held in May, promoted by Skegness Aero Club on the airfield near the Royal Oak Hotel, Roman Bank. Said to be the first of its kind in the area, it attracted 15,000 spectators. Skegness Aerodrome had been opened a year earlier by Capt. G.A. Pennington and Michael Scott who provided five-shilling (25p) trips over the town in a three-seater Puss Moth monoplane.

MOTOR LIFEBOAT. In December the last of the rowing and sailing lifeboats, the Samuel Lewis, was replaced by the motor lifeboat, Anne Allen, the crew being reduced from 15 to 8 members as a result.

LUMLEY SECONDARY SCHOOL opened by Lindsey County Council on October 17. Headmaster Harry Bamber and most of his staff moved from the National School, Roman Bank, which had closed down.

LUMLEY SQUARE reconstructed and old houses near the Cricket Ground demolished.

1933   CYCLING CLUB. Skegness Wheelers C.C. formed on 23 February. Cycling, hiking and youth-hostelling were really taking off at this period and the Wheelers quickly became one of the most popular outdoor organisations in the area.

SUN CASTLE opened at Easter as a Solarium with ultra-violet ray lamps for artificial sun-bathing. Needing special protective clothing, it never became popular and, after only a few seasons, the lamps were removed and the building was utilised for light refreshments accompanied by a musical trio. The official opening ceremony had been performed the previous Christmas by Sir Leonard Hill.

1933 SUNDAY TRIPPERS. Skegness Council received a petition from local hotel and boardinghouse keepers requesting them to take immediate steps to stop the invasion of weekend trippers whose rowdy behaviour was losing them their staying visitors. No action was taken.

PARADE CINEMA, Grand Parade, opened just before Christmas, owned by R.L.Kemp of Nottingham.

CENTRAL HALL, Roman Bank, became the Central Cinema, also opening for Christmas. The roof of the building had to be raised several feet to accommodate the cinematograph equipment.

FORESHORE MANAGEMENT. Skegness UD Council appointed its first foreshore manager in the person of H.L.Dodsworth who had held a similar post at Tynemouth. Until that date the foreshore undertaking came under the Surveyor's Department with a sands inspector.

SEWERAGE. Skegness Council built a new sewage disposal works on Burgh Marsh with full land treatment, known as the Middlemarsh Sewerage Works.

CAREY HOUSE CONVALESCENT HOME for Women opened on Roman Bank, Seathorne. It was named after Miss Henrietta Carey who had been closely associated with the Nottinghamshire Men's Convalescent Home on an adjoining site.

WASH SPEEDWAY scheme finally abandoned after the promoters went into liquidation. Launched in 1929, it envisaged an international motor racing track on the mudflats between Boston and Gibraltar Point with an aerodrome and other facilities.

SKEGNESS GRAMMAR SCHOOL opened in September, costing £35,000, and replacing the Magdalen College School at Wainfleet whose headmaster, K.G. Spendlove, MA., took charge of the new County Council school.

CARNIVAL. The first of the huge street processions organised by Billy Butlin, with massive band contests, this year attracting about seventy competing bands. The Butlin annual carnivals continued until 1937.

ST. MATTHEW'S CHURCH choir vestry added to the west end of the building.

SKEGNESS BOWLING CLUB opened their new bowling greens in Briar Close, after 29 years at the Lumley Hotel.

WOODSIDE HOLIDAY CAMP (established in Grosvenor Road with tents in 1920) replaced with permanent buildings, still under the ownership of the YMCA. Costing £12,000, it had accommodation for 450 visitors.

VERGER. The rector, Canon A.H.Morris, reported to the Parochial Church Council that, following the death of Mr. Percy Rowe, 85 applications had been received to fill the office of verger. Only the 22 local applications were considered and Mr.H.Scott was appointed.

1934 LAWN CINEMA closed in February and the main building was incorporated in Hildreds Hotel, with shops fronting the public lavatories in Lumley Road.

WINTER GARDENS CIRCUS, North Parade, inaugurated by Arthur Joel which ran each summer until war commenced. Arthur Joel died in 1950, aged sixty-eight.

CASTLETON BOULEVARD opened as a dual-carriageway to provide a direct route from Burgh Road to the seafront. The scheme incorporated Skegness's first traffic lights.

GAS SHOWROOMS and new public lavatories opened in Lumley Square on site of old cottages demolished a year earlier.

ST. CLEMENT'S CHURCH , the former Skegness parish church, after years of decay, reopened for services, on the initiative of the rector, Canon Arthur H.Morris.

MARINE MUSEUM. Skegness Council proposed to add a first floor to the Cafe Dansant, Tower Esplanade, to accommodate James Giles's local collection of artifacts, etc. which he had promised to give to the Council if they would provide a suitable exhibition building. It was estimated that the building alterations would cost £1,330 but the work was never put in hand.

FORESHORE CENTRE, Tower Esplanade, converted from the Cafe Dansant to accommodate the Council's new Foreshore Department and other public facilities.

GRAND NATIONAL runner, Delaneige, sent by his trainer, George Beeby, to prepare for the big race on Skegness sands. The horse ran second to the winner, Golden Miller.

TOWN BUS SERVICE, operated by the Stinson brothers' Skegness Motor Service Company, taken over by Lincolnshire Road Car Co. Ltd. The latter was formed in 1928, largely by the railway companies, and they eventually bought out most of the small bus operators in the county.

1935　　　SKEGNESS COUNTY JUNIOR SCHOOL opened off Cavendish Road.

SILVER JUBILEE of the Coronation of King George V and Queen Mary celebrated in May, coinciding with the Whitsun weekend. The weather was fine, streets were decorated, the clock tower illuminated and thousands of visitors added to the carnival atmosphere. Local children were given free teas and free rides in the amusement parks, games in the Tower Gardens, finishing with a huge bonfire and fireworks display on the beach.

COUNTY HOTEL, North Parade, opened in June by Bateman's Brewery of Wainfleet.

SKEGNESS EXCELSIOR BAND formed, mainly from disaffected members of the Salvation Army Band, including bandmaster Albert Petch. They enjoyed considerable success until disbanded during the war.

CRICKET. South Africa tourists played the Minor Counties on the Cricket Ground, the three day match drawing about four thousand spectators. The tourists won by eight wickets.

PIER SALE. Skegness UD Council discussed the purchase of the pier with the Earl of Scarbrough, but after a survey and report the local authority decided to take no action. The Earl had offered to negotiate with the Council in 1927, but nothing came of it then.

1936　　　SHIP HOTEL, with public entrances on Roman Bank and Burgh Road, demolished. The public house had opened in 1856, at that time just inside Winthorpe parish. The pub was replaced by a new Ship Hotel, just across the road, when Castleton Boulevard opened.

BUTLIN'S HOLIDAY CAMP opened during a very cold Easter, although only partly completed. Situated on Roman Bank, it was just over the boundary in Ingoldmells parish.

AUGUST BANK HOLIDAY said to be a record up to that date with an estimated 135,000 visitors on the Monday.

JOHN HASSALL (1868-1948), creator of the Jolly Fisherman poster, made his first and only recorded visit to the resort he had helped to make famous. He came at the invitation of the Skegness Advancement Association (the body responsible for town publicity) who presented him with an illuminated address from the Council and granted him 'the freedom of the foreshore.'

SCOUTS' HALL, Wainfleet Road - named St. George's Hall - officially opened by Deputy Chief Scout, Sir Percy Everitt.

SKEGNESS COUNCIL OF CHRISTIAN CHURCHES formed.

GERMAN ZEPPELIN, Hindenberg, seen flying over Skegness. One witness was Sir John Marsden the Grimsby 'trawler king',who saw it from his house on Seacroft Esplanade. Sir John's allegations that the Germans were using it for spying received considerable publicity in the national press.

SKEGNESS HOTELIERS' ASSOCIATION formed in early December, the same month King Edward VIII abdicated and George VI became king.

SHEEPDOG TRIALS held on the Seacroft Esplanade foreshore in June, but spoilt by wet weather.

1937   WARD SYSTEM introduced, Skegness being divided into North and South Wards for electoral purposes, increasing the Urban District Council's members from 15 to 18. The new arrangement also allowed Skegness two county councillors instead of one.

MARKS & SPENCER opened a branch in Lumley Road on the site of the former Greenwood's Cafe. The store began business on June 4, with nothing priced above five shillings (25p).

PIER ENTRANCE reconstructed in contemporary art deco style, retaining the central steps, but blocking in the attractive ballustrading along the two ramps.

CATTLE MARKET, Albert Road, closed down on September 30, on retirement of proprietor George Frederick Ball.

LION TRAGEDY. The ex-rector of Stiffkey, Norfolk, Harold Davidson, fatally mauled by a lion on July 28 whilst performing with Fred Rye's lions in the Pleasureland amusement park at Seaview Pullover.

BUTLIN COMPANY FLOATED. W.E.Butlin's various companies covering amusement parks, a holiday camp and other enterprises, combined in Butlin's Ltd. with authorised share capital of £220,000. Mr. Butlin was to continue as managing director with a salary of £3,000 per annum. It was stated that Butlin amusement parks were opened at Skegness in 1927, Mablethorpe 1928, Bognor Regis 1930, Felixstow, Hayling Island, Southsea and Littlehampton 1931 and the Skegness holiday camp in 1936.

SKEGNESS PLAYGOERS SOCIETY formed at a meeting held on November 24 on the initiative of Frank Smith and Eric Heard, Dr. Allan presiding. The last-named - father of film star Elizabeth Allan - was appointed president, with Eric Heard, secretary and it was decided to hold the first play reading at the Arcadia Theatre in January.

1938	LUMLEY ROAD DUAL-CARRIAGEWAY constructed at the eastern end and opened in April.

SCARBROUGH ESPLANADE opened, one of its main purposes being to serve as a slipway for launching the lifeboat, although it was never used as such.

WATERWAY extended from the pier to Tower Esplanade.

ST. MATTHEW'S CHURCH began to sink on its foundations, in serious danger of collapse. Powlett Circus was closed to traffic whilst expensive remedial work was carried out. The cause was said to be inadequate foundations and the lowering of the water table when paving was laid around the building.

BANDSTAND in front of the Tower Gardens Pavilion demolished, not having been used for a number of years.

GEORGE ROBEY', 'prime minister of mirth,' did a one-night show at the King's Theatre, whilst Gracie Fields sang at Butlin's Holiday Camp to a reported audience of several thousand.

TOWN MUSEUM. James Giles, long-time resident, businessman and amateur antiquarian, again offered to give the Council his large collection of local artefacts if they would provide a suitable place for their exhibition. The Council had agreed to do this four years earlier but no further steps were taken. Mr. Giles died soon afterwards and his collection was sold by auction and dispersed.

SKEGNESS CHRYSANTHEMUM SOCIETY formed and held its first annual show.

GAS MASKS issued for every resident in the town, following the deteriorating situation in Germany.

WOMEN'S VOLUNTARY SERVICE. A Skegness branch established the same year the national organisation came into being.

ARP. Different section of the Air Raids Precautions service formed, with the control centre at Pembroke House, Rutland Road (now the Masonic Hall).

KINGS THEATRE AND SWIMMING BATHS, Scarbrough Avenue, purchased by R.L.Kemp's Skegness Entertainments Ltd. who already owned the three cinemas, Arcadia Theatre and the Winter Gardens, giving the Nottingham company a monopoly of the resort's entertainments.

1939   BUTLIN'S HOLIDAY CAMP suffered extensive damage in two massive fires within a week during February. The camp was closed at the time and the conflagrations were said to be the work of arsonists. Mr. Butlin had no doubt about it. The fires destroyed restaurants and other buildings fronting Roman Bank, but reconstruction began immediately and the camp was in full working order for Easter.

DERBYSHIRE MINERS' WELFARE HOLIDAY CAMP, Winthorpe Avenue, opened in May, said to be the first miners' holiday camp in Britain.

HOSPITAL EXTENSIONS. Skegness & District Hospital underwent major extensions, including a maternity ward, and was formally opened on 25 May by HRH the Duchess of Gloucester.

RESORT PUBLICITY. L. & N. E. Rly. launched 'the most intensive campaign ever undertaken' to popularise the Lincolnshire resorts (with the slogan, 'Meet the sun on the East Coast.'

FOOTBALL. The two top local teams, Skegness United and Skegness Blue Rovers, met each other for the last time in the final of the Skegness Nursing Cup, the Blues winning 2-1 on April 22. The two clubs never reformed after the war. Skegness Thursday FC finished the 1938-39 season as champions of the Boston Thursday League.

CRICKET. A celebrity match on the Richmond Drive ground, arranged for September 3-4, cancelled owing to the outbreak of war. The touring West Indies team had been booked to play W.E.Butlin's XI which included Jack Hobbs, Patsy Hendren, Frank Woolley, Maurice Tate, George Duckworth and Andy Sandham, all England internationals.

WAR DECLARED by prime minister Neville Chamberlain in a radio broadcast on Sunday morning, September 3. The Skegness summer season came to an abrupt end and, although the expected air raids did not materialise at once, the resident population was quickly reduced by men and women joining the armed forces or leaving to work in armaments factories inland, particularly the MARCO ammunition works in Grantham. Skegness Council and local building firms were engaged to construct defence works, including concrete tank traps on the pullovers leading to the beaches and bases for six-inch gun batteries at Jackson's Corner, Roman Bank, and Gibraltar Point. They were later to carry out repairs to bombed properties as far along the coast as Mablethorpe. The ARP service - later renamed Civil Defence - was strengthened with fire-watchers stationed in business premises to deal with incendiary bombs and air-raid wardens patrolling the streets on the lookout for houses showing chinks of light through their blackout curtains and blinds. The Army took control of the beaches and

1939 minefields were laid in some areas with rolls of barbed wire keeping away friend and foe alike, but on different sides of the wire. As in the First World War, Gibraltar Point was occupied by the military and rifle ranges and other practice facilities were constructed. A company of Local Defence Volunteers (LDV) - later called the Home Guard - quickly enlisted to full strength and the regular army established searchlight and radar posts in the neighbourhood. A Royal Observer Corps observation post was also well manned keeping tabs on all aircraft approaching the area. Residents remaining in the town, adults and children, went about their business carrying little cardboard boxes containing their gas masks. Food was rationed and not many people were bothered with overweight problems.

BANANA BRIGADE. A light ant-aircraft unit was formed from local volunteers, nicknamed the 'Banana Brigade' because their headquarters was Hercock's former wholesale banana warehouse in High Street. The unit was drafted to India and saw active service as part of 106 Light AA Battery.

EVACUEES. Many children from Grimsby were brought to Skegness almost immediately war was declared as it was considered, quite erroneously as it turned out, a safe area. The children were assembled in the Tower Gardens where they were collected by temporary foster parents, but a number returned home during the period of 'the phoney war' before the real action started. The foster parents were paid 10s.6d. (52p) per week for food and care for each child, reduced to 8s.6d. (42p) for two or more.

BUTLIN'S HOLIDAY CAMP was quickly taken over by the Admiralty to become HMS Royal Arthur (named after a cruiser built in 1891) for the training of recruits for the Royal Navy. In addition, there were trainees from the free forces of Norway and several other countries, numbering at any one time something like four thousand men. Most of them, it can be imagined, trod the concrete decks of Royal Arthur with rueful smiles as they glanced up at the large letters of the Butlin camp slogan, 'Our true intent is all for your delight.' That first winter of the war was the coldest in living memory and the rookie sailors were housed in flimsy wooden chalets with no heating.

1940 SNOW. Adding to the problems of war, heavy snowfalls with gale force winds blocked railway and road, completely isolating Skegness for several days in January-February. Bad weather was nationwide and was said to be the worst winter for a hundred years.

DEFENCE ZONE regulations closed all beaches to the public, but concessions later granted to Skegness, as well as other resorts, allowed entry during daylight hours. The pier also closed for the duration.

BEAM WIRELESS STATION at Winthorpe, whose eight tall masts could be seen across the Wash, dismantled because of danger to planes.

1940   AIR RAID SHELTERS. Communal air raid shelters were erected on the grass verges in Lumley Avenue and Scarbrough Avenue, with brick walls and thick flat concrete roofs. Until recent years the concrete floors remained in situ. None of the popular Anderson corrugated iron shelters were provided as they required deep ground excavation, rendered difficult by the area's high water table. Instead, Morrison indoor shelters were made available. They consisted of four legs of heavy angle iron, supporting a table top of sheet steel with wire mesh sides. Below was sleeping space for two people. The shelter parts were delivered by the Council to each applicant for self-assembly.

BOMBING. The first bombs on Skegness were incendiaries, falling on the Seacroft golf links about 1.15 a.m. on July 23. The first high explosives also fell on the same links, about midnight on August 19, in both cases causing little damage. On August 21, about midday, HEs dropped in the grounds of the NDFS convalescent home, North Parade and a gas main near the County Hotel was set on fire. An hour later, bombs in Richmond Drive moved a pair of Council houses off their foundations, whilst the raider followed up dropping more bombs near the gasworks, one falling between two gasholders. One enemy plane was shot down in the sea and three others destroyed by RAF fighters in the Alford area. A further raid the same day resulted in three killed and 38 injured at HMS Royal Arthur.

Park Avenue, Glentworth Crescent and North Parade were bombed on August 23 when five houses were destroyed and two small children died. The cattle market was hit on the afternoon of October 3 and bombs also fell on the Royal Arthur. There were a number of other less serious raids during the year.

On October 9, Spitfires shot down a Junkers 88 in the sea, but earlier in the year, on March 4, Wing Commander Guy Gibson, flying a Beaufighter from RAF Digby, shot down a night raider a short distance off the pierhead. Next day, the famous Dambuster leader came over with some of his lads to collect the Heinkel's propeller.

BOMBERS' GATEWAY, Skegness pier was a well defined landmark for RAF bombers crossing the coast to and from Germany and, writing in Lincolnshire Life magazine in September 1982, Sqdn. Ldr. G.Haworth, DFC, DFM, recalled happy trips to the resort when stationed at Waddington RAF, near Lincoln. When war came however, Skegness 'was immediately designated as the route by which bombers were compelled to leave and enter the county. For several long years, Skegness served as a gateway to the North Sea and many parts of Europe, and also provided thousands of airmen with the last sight of England they were ever going to see.'

Sqdn. Ldr. Haworth flew Lancasters over Skegness many times in the war years, using the pier, pointing like a long finger. to guide them towards the enemy coast over the sea. Many others found it a welcome sight as their damaged aircraft limped home looking for a safe landing place.

1941 RAF SKEGNESS opened on 11 February 1941 and within a month its total strength was just on 3,000. The following year it reached a maximum of 7,000. Most of the vacant private hotels and other buildings were taken over and when accommodation was exhausted an additional wing had to be opened in Boston. Headquarters was at the Seacroft Hotel and the Imperial Cafe, the Casino and Tower Gardens Pavilion provided messrooms. The former Seacroft Boys' School, Seacroft Esplanade was the main sick quarters. Drilling took place on Tower Esplanade, in the car parks and side streets and firing practice at Gibraltar Point and on the beach where it was not mined or excluded by barbed wire. RAF Skegness, or No.11 RAF Recruit Training Centre, closed down in October 1944 and by that time it had provided initial training for about 80,000 airmen.

BOMBING. One of the town's worst air raids occurred about 4 pm on Saturday, January 18, when a single enemy plane came over low from the land near dusk, possibly attracted by a shop window light. It dropped a string of 14 bombs along the eastern end of Lumley Road, tailing off along Tower Esplanade. One fell on the Tower Cinema where a matinee was in progress, but none of the children were injured, although the building was almost wrecked. The bomb had exploded on impact with the roof otherwise the effect would have been horrific. Councillor O.K. Morgan, an accountant, was killed in his office and Charles Hershberg died in his cafe, struck by flying glass. Many buildings were damaged, but the clock tower suffered only splintered brickwork although one of the bombs fell close by on the Lumley Road side.

The Algitha Road Methodist Church suffered severe damage in a raid about 2 am on February 16 and the pair of large houses on its east side were completely destroyed. On April 17, just before midnight, HEs fell on the Church Hall, Ida Road, and the nearby police station. The former was being used as the First Aid depot, but nobody was injured in either building. Another bomb fell on a platform at the railway station.

On May 10 a little boy was killed when a bomb fell in Saxby Avenue and on June 14 Dean's Farm, Wainfleet Road, was seriously damaged and one man died in the early morning raid. Other attacks during the year caused only minor damage at Coronation Walk, the boating lake, Burgh Road brickworks, in fields and on the beach. A raider was shot down in the sea on March 13 and another one the following day after dropping incendiaries over a wide area.

On October 11, Skegness lifeboat picked up five airmen in a dinghy, the crew of a Whitley bomber which crashed in the sea, eleven miles SE of the pier, returning from Germany.

WHALE ASHORE. A whale carcase, said to be a Lesser Rorqual, washed ashore near Sea View pullover and, after much debate about who was responsible for its disposal and agitation about the polluted atmosphere in that area, it was cut up and moved by local butchers.

1942 BOMBING. North Parade was attacked about 1.30 pm on February 2, bombs landing in the grounds of the NDFS Convalescent Home (later the Town Hall) and on the Pier Sports Field. Another dropped in front of Miss Blanchard's cafe under the pier where a number of people were enjoying a meal, but it failed to explode. On February 21, about 10 am, HEs fell on Vine Road and Norwood Road, destroying one house and damaging others; another house had to be demolished to excavate an unexploded bomb. The same raider attacked Royal Arthur, killing four and injuring fourteen naval personnel.

In Lumley Avenue, on July 27, under cover of early morning mist, a plane came in from the sea, seriously damaging a number of houses and killing seven people, including a mother and daughter. Incendiaries fell near the Arcadia Theatre around midnight on September 15 and nearby Kimberley House in Drummond Road was flattened by HE bombs. Another bomb left a large crater on the Lumley Road side of the clock tower, whilst incendiaries set fire to a house on Grand Parade, causing three deaths, the firefighters being hindered when the water supply was cut off. The first 'flowerpot' incendiaries dropped at Gibraltar Point on September 15.

Skegness's last and worst single raid of the whole war occurred on October 24 at 9.45 pm The high explosives fell near the junction of Scarbrough Avenue and Park Avenue, together with 'flowerpot' incendiaries. Ten buildings, including the Red House Hotel, were almost totally destroyed, another house was set on fire and had to be demolished and some 300 other buildings suffered damage. Twelve people died and 66 were injured.

AIR TRAINING CORPS. Skegness Flight 1073 Squadron ATC formed.

SKEGNESS SEA CADETS formed _. .

1943 STORM TIME. A northerly gale and high tide in April caused flooding from Mablethorpe to Skegness. At Mablethorpe and Sutton water invaded the High Streets, houses had to be evacuated in Chapel St.Leonards, whilst at Skegness the sea came up Tower Esplanade.

WARTIME RESTRICTIONS eased when the beach was reopened to the public, from May to September, between 6 am and 9 pm.

	LIFEBOAT picked up two bodies on January 21, 1½ miles south of the pier after a collision between a Lysander and a Spitfire. On June 27, two airmen were rescued from a rubber dinghy 6 miles north-east of the pier.
1944	BEACH MINES. A twenty year old sapper of the Royal Engineers was killed clearing a minefield on Skegness beach.
	LUMLEY ROAD RECONSTRUCTION DREAM. Discussions took place between Skegness Urban District Council and Lindsey County Council concerning a post war scheme sweeping away all the property on the south side of Lumley Road, from Keightley's Stores to Tonglet's Corner, and the north side of High Street to leave a 70 ft. wide carriageway and 25 ft. sidewalks, 'costing half a million.' The County Council was willing to take the matter to the Ministry of Transport, but Skegness Council 'changed their minds.' (Skegness Standard, 15.11.44.)
1945	LIGHTS COME ON AGAIN. A limited number of street lights were switched on in August, the first time since war began.
	WARTIME RECORDS. Police statistics, published in 1945, disclosed that during the course of the war, bombs totally destroyed 38 buildings in Skegness, 75 others were seriously damaged and 1,282 received minor damage. Another source revealed that Skegness Lifeboat logged 70 incidents (including standbys) involving planes crashing into the sea during the period of hostilities and many lives were saved.
	SKEGNESS TOWN FC formed at a public meeting on December 13 at St. George's Hall, Wainfleet Road, under chairmanship of Cllr. A.E. Fletcher, Skegness Standard editor, who had been connected with Skegness football for forty years.
	RAOB CLUB, Briar Way, became Skegness Working Men's Club and Institute in March.
1946	SKEGNESS THURSDAY FC. reformed at a meeting in February after suspending activity for the duration of the war.
	COUNCIL HOUSING. Work commenced on the first post-war Skegness Council house building with 64 dwellings as the first stage of the Winthorpe Housing Estate. The Ministry of Health rejected tenders of local building contractors as too high and the UDC then decided to carry out the work by direct labour.
	LAWN MOTOR PARK, between Briar Way and Beresford Avenue, opened for cars and coaches.

BUTLIN'S AMUSEMENT PARK on south side of pier. As the lease expired, Skegness UD Council would only renew it on a year-to-year basis, pending agreement to modernise and refurbish the attractions. The agreed rental was £8,000, plus rates.

ROYAL BRITISH LEGION county rally, marking their Silver Jubilee, held on Sunday, June 30, Nearly five thousand legionnaires from 113 Lincolnshire branches, with several bands, marched from the Pier Field to the Cricket Ground and three packed trains and a large number of coaches brought supporters from all over the county.

ROYAL AIR FORCE ASSOCIATION. A Skegness branch was formed at a meeting in the Marine Hotel in November. The organisation held monthly meetings and reached a peak of about 150 members and Mrs Lillian Streets, a founder member of the branch, was hon sec. for 35 years. (The Association closed in 2006 with a farewell lunch in 2006, its diamond jubilee year.)

1947　　SEA FRUIT. Hundreds of crates of grapefruit washed ashore, mostly still edible, attracting hordes of beachcombers to the coast (Feb.).

PIER glazed over at the landward end to form an amusement arcade.

PLAYING FIELDS, to be known as the War Memorial Playing Fields, Wainfleet Road, opened for sports activities. They were taken over by Skegness UDC in 1951.

SKEGNESS AIRFIELD, off Skegness Road, Ingoldmells, opened on land owned by Butlin's. Short pleasure trips over the town were operated and Skegness Aero Club was also based there. The club had been founded in 1931, using the Royal Oak airfield on Roman Bank which had closed at the outbreak of war.

LIBRARY. Skegness County Library moved from the Town Hall to fresh premises at 23, Roman Bank, formerly Rowley's furniture stores, The new library opened on October 1, for the first time with a full time staff, open every weekday.

1948　　CLEMENT ATTLEE attended the annual rally of the Lincolnshire branch of the National Union of Agricultural Workers held on Sunday June 27. Led by Skegness Town Band and Spalding Town Band, they marched from the Pier Field to Princes Parade where the prime minister addressed the gathering.

BOXING tournament held on the Cricket Ground on September 8th when Jimmy Wilde, the great Welsh former flyweight champion of the world, was introduced and displayed his original gold Lonsdale Belt. Bruce Woodcock, British and European heavyweight champion, boxed a three round exhibition bout with a Canadian heavyweight. Promoted by Cllr. Reuben Rowe, the programme included several local boxers and was well supported.

JOHN HASSALL, creator of the famous Skegness Jolly Fisherman poster in 1908, died at the age of eighty.

SKEGNESS & DISTRICT HOSPITAL, after 35 years as a voluntary service, became part of the new National Health Service, as from July 5.

PIER DIVERS. The high-diving platform on the pier removed to make way for a new bar. The divers had performed there since the 1890s, the last one being 'Daredevil Leslie' Gadsby who succeeded his father, 'Peggy' Gadsby, a one-legged diver.

NORTH BRACING, formerly Marine Walk, reconstructed from Tower Esplanade to the Pier and connecting to the Sports Field (later Pier Field), opening on July 28. The walk had originally been built in 1930

PIER THEATRE, at the pierhead, reconstructed from what had been the Pavilion, and earlier, the Saloon. Launched with a civic opening at Whitsun.

GIBRALTAR POINT. Lincolnshire Trust for Nature Conservation formed in December and, a week later, signed an agreement with Lindsey County Council to lease land for the nature reserve.

SKEGNESS RUGBY CLUB formed at a meeting at the Links Hotel on February 24 when J.A.C.Baker-Beall was elected secretary, being the prime mover of the initiative. Col. T.E.Pearman, CBE., became the first president.

1949 PENSIONERS' ASSEMBLY HALL, Alexandra Road, opened.

SOUTH BRACING completed in time for season, running southward from Tower Esplanade to Princes Parade

STORM. In early March, what was said to be the heaviest storms in living memory saw the sea overflowing into the boating lake. The new South Bracing was wrecked and completion delayed and serious damage occurred at Mablethorpe, Sutton and Chapel, whilst in Boston the Witham flooded the Stump.

SKEGNESS TOWN FC finished eleventh out of fourteen teams in the first season of the Lincolnshire League. (The following season they were runners-up to Brigg Town, after signing several part-time professionals as the other teams had done.)

DUKE OF EDINBURGH visited Butlin's Camp in September to receive a cheque for £5,000 for the National Playing Fields Association.

FIRE AT CAMP. The Derbyshire Miners' Holiday Centre devastated by fire which destroyed the wooden theatre and dining hall. They were later replaced by brick buildings.

1950 BARROW BOYS. Skegness Taxi Proprietors' Association sent a letter to Skegness UD Council asking them to request the police to 'put a stop' to the barrow boys touting for luggage on Saturday mornings as they were a pest and were seriously affecting the taxi drivers' living. After consulting the police, the Council replied that as no complaints for obstruction by barrow boys had been received no action could be taken.

ROMAN CATHOLIC CHURCH opened by Bishop of Nottingham on July 30, replacing the old church on the adjoining site in Grosvenor Road, built in 1898. The new church was built of locally manufactured bricks by Skegness building contractors, William Greetham & Son, who owned the Burgh Road Brick Works.

SEACROFT CHURCH. At the Parochial Church Council meeting on August 15 it was suggested by Mr. M.Backwell that a committee be appointed to look into the possibility of obtaining land to build a church at Seacroft. Nothing resulted from the investigation.

SKEGNESS ROUND TABLE branch formed in November.

SEACROFT SPECIAL SCHOOL for Girls opened by Lindsey County Council in the former Seacroft Preparatory School on Seacroft Esplanade. In Skegness, the latter was more frequently referred to as Sparrow's School, after the headmaster and proprietor, H.E.Sparrow, MA. The school had opened just before, or just after, the First World War with the declared purpose to 'provide a good education for the sons of gentlemen so as to fit them in work and character for the Public Schools or the Royal Navy.' It closed at the outbreak of the Second World War, whilst the Special School for Girls shut down in 1984. The large building, overlooking the shore, has been a private nursing home for some years.

LIBRARY. Skegness County Library, 23, Roman Bank, after closure for complete refurbishment, reopened early in the year. As the district library, the Skegness branch was also responsible for the administration and staffing of the part-time branches at Wainfleet, Burgh and Spilsby.

1951 FESTIVAL PAVILION (later Festival Centre) opened in July as Skegness's commemoration of the Festival of Britain. It was built primarily as an open-air roller skating rink with facilities for concerts and other activities.

TOWER CINEMA reopened after disastrous damage in an air-raid in 1941. An entirely new frontage and many internal alterations had been carried out in the rebuilding.

STREET LIGHTING. Conversion from gas to electricity commenced

SKEGNESS LEAGUE OF FRIENDS formed in December to provide financial support for Skegness & District Hospital, the Isolation Hospital at Wainfleet Road, and Seely House and Carey House Convalescent Homes at Seathorne. (In Dec., 2000, when the Friends celebrated their fiftieth anniversary, nearly £70,000 had been raised.)

WOMEN'S INSTITUTE, WINTHORPE BRANCH. Mrs. Ivy Tagg of Roydene Farm, Winthorpe, called a meeting on September 11 at which 23 ladies formed the Winthorpe Branch of the W.I. At a further meeting, on November 9, 44 members were enrolled and Mrs. Tagg was elected president and Mrs Gardiner secretary. A committee was also elected and other arrangements made.

1952 CORONATION OF QUEEN ELIZABETH II. Cllr. George Swaby, chairman of the UD Council, read the proclamation from the balcony of the Town Hall and, on Coronation Day, there were children's treats, bonfire, street procession and other events.

GIBRALTAR POINT declared a Local Nature Reserve under the National Parks Act, 1949, by Lindsey County Council and Skegness Urban District Council. (The 50th. anniversary of the statutory declaration was celebrated in August 2002.)

SEATHORNE COUNTY PRIMARY SCHOOL opened 15 March by Lindsey County Council. Headmaster was H.S. ('Snowy') Gardiner with 5 staff and 154 pupils. The new school replaced Winthorpe village school - opened in 1865 - which closed at the same time.

MURPHY RADIO opened a factory in the Winter Gardens, North Parade.

1953 EAST COAST FLOOD, on the Saturday night of 31 January, caused terrible destruction all along the Lincolnshire coast and southward. Skegness was fortunate to escape with no loss of life and only heavy damage to the foreshore non-residential area. The high and wide beach absorbed much of the wave force, causing them to break further offshore. The sea flooded the Compass Gardens, the Embassy Theatre and the Sun Castle, with many other buildings wrecked or swept away, but the old stone parade wall held fast. Sixteen lives were lost in neighbouring Ingoldmells.

ANEURIN BEVAN, the cabinet minister who had pushed through the National Health Service, addressed the annual union rally of the Lincolnshire agricultural workers at Skegness on June 21.

TOWER GARDENS FAIRYLAND held from 11 July to 19 October when the gardens were filled with giant set pieces. Entrances were closed during the period of the illuminations, except the paybox at the Grand Parade gateway, the admission charge being one shilling (5p) with children half price. Strip lights and floodlights lit up the parades and boating lake and Lumley Road, drawing large crowds of visitors. The Tower Gardens Fairyland was switched on by television celebrity 'grumpy' Gilbert Harding, The Lumley Road and foreshore illuminations had been inaugurated as early as 1932, but suspended when war began and not reinstated until 1953. 'Fairyland' was a financial failure and not repeated, but the foreshore illuminations continued as a major annual attraction, with a show-biz or sports personality performing the switch-on ceremony in the Clock Tower area.

SEACROFT RAILWAY STATION closed to passenger traffic in November, after eighty years) but goods traffic continued until April 1964.

1954   KINGS THEATRE AND INDOOR SWIMMING BATHS. Destroyed by wartime bombing, the site in Scarbrough Avenue purchased from United Entertainments Ltd. by Skegness UDC for £12,500. The payment was largely covered by compensation received from the War Damage Commission and the Council agreed not to use the land for a cinema, circus or variety entertainment, competing with the vendors. After clearing the ground it was put to use as a temporary car park, which eventually became permanent.

ROSE BROS. (GAINSBOROUGH) LTD. opened an engineering works on Church Road South.

WHITE SEAL washed ashore at Gibraltar Point, nearly 9 ft. in length. After about twelve hours ashore it swam off on the rising tide.

1955   DROWNING TRAGEDY. On a Sunday afternoon in February, three lives were lost on the frozen brickpit off Wainfleet Road. Seven year old Raymond Key was with his dog as it ran onto the ice and when it broke the boy ran out to rescue it and also fell into the water. Another boy who was with him hurried to fetch help from Raymond's nearby home and his 40 year old mother, Mrs. Annie Key, and daughter Beryl (18) rushed to the scene and both were drowned in an attempted rescue.

TOWN PUBLICITY. Council foreshore manager Willan G.Bosworth redesignated director of foreshore, entertainments and publicity as Skegness UDC took over town advertising from Skegness Advancement Association who had carried out that function for many years and, since the war, with a full-time secretary.

DIESEL TRAINS began running on the Skegness - Boston line.

NORTH PARADE SPORTS GROUND (Pier Field) on the north side of the pier, pressed into service as an emergency car park at Whitsun weekend, thereafter being used regularly for that purpose.

SKEGNESS & DISTRICT PIG CLUB, said to be Skegness's oldest institution, reported minimal membership at its 85th. annual meeting and closed down soon afterwards. The club had been formed when many residents kept a pig and members were insured for compensation should their pig die from natural causes.

FOOTBALL. Skegness Town, after beating Grantham and Gainsborough Trinity in the Qualifying Rounds, became the first Lincolnshire League club to reach the 1st Round proper of the FA Cup. They were then defeated 4-0 by Worksop Town on the Burgh Road Ground. The gate was recorded as 3,860. (In the following round, Boston United beat Derby County 6-1.)

1956 BLIZZARD. Beginning early on Sunday morning, January 8, heavy snowfalls and gale force northerly winds swept across the country. Electricity and telephone cables and wires were brought down and Skegness was cut off for light and power and communications. Deep snow blocked the roads and railway and guttering over Lumley Road shops clattered to the pavement, many premises being roped off for safety. The thaw began after a week of great hardship, bringing burst pipes and flooding.

HUNGARIAN RISING brought about twelve hundred refugees to Skegness to be provided with temporary shelter at the Derbyshire Miners' Holiday Centre and the YMCA Holiday Camp. Arriving in December, most were dispersed by the following April to find work inland.

ROCK AND ROLL hit the country and when the film, 'Rock Around the Clock,' was screened at the Parade Cinema, hundreds of teenagers danced frenziedly in the building and in the street outside, having to be dispersed by the police. A jazz club was organised by Harry Segal and opened by Benny Hill soon afterwards.

TEDDY BOYS and Hells Angels had gang fights on August Bank Holiday, requiring police reinforcements. For several summers afterwards, gangs on motorcycles caused much disruption at weekends, gathering in large numbers on Grand Parade and in Lumley Road.

WELCOME INN opened by Shipstone's on Old Burgh Road.

1957 WHALE, 21 ft. long, washed ashore alive at Gibraltar Point. A killer whale, it died despite desperate efforts to get it refloated.

MORRIS SECONDARY SCHOOL Church Road North, opened by Lindsey County Council, costing £130,000. The School was named after former rector, the much loved Canon, Arthur H.Morris.

THE HORSE AND CART ERA ended for Skegness Council when they retired their last two horses. The large stable building at the Council Depot was converted for other purposes and carts, harness and other accessories sold off. When the Council proposed to send the two old servants to the knacker's yard there was a public outcry and, in the end, arrangements were made for Captain and Brandy to be put out to pasture on a farm in the Wolds.

1958   LEICESTER TO SKEGNESS WALK instituted and won by a 34 year old Leicester bricklayer who covered the 100 miles in 18h.2m.37s. The event was promoted by Leicester Walking Club and the newly-formed Skegness Athletic Club, but the latter organisation had only a short existence.

GIBRALTAR POINT. The former Coastguard Station building, disused since the early 1900s, acquired by Lindsey County Council and leased to the Lincolnshire Naturalists' Trust to become their field station. The building had been occupied by the Army in the Second World War.

SKEGNESS TOWN FC. elected to the Midland Counties League, one of the strongest outside the Football League. At that date a number of clubs, including Boston United, defected to the Southern League and the vacancies were filled by Skegness Town and several clubs from the north-east, including Ashington, Blyth Spartans and North Shields. The Lilywhites finished sixth in their first season, behind leaders Peterborough United who were soon promoted to the Football League. The following season, after Skegness finished twelfth, the Midland League closed down and Town joined the Central Alliance League.

It was also in 1958 the town club purchased the Burgh Road ground - where they had played since 1947 - from the Earl of Scarbrough.

1959   GEORGE, RAYNOR (1907-85), famous football manager who had settled in Skegness, appointed to take charge of Skegness Town FC. A former Sheffield United player and Coventry City manager, he had coached Sweden amateurs to win the 1948 Olympic title. They later invited him back to coach the Sweden international team and in 1958 he took them to the World Cup Final where they were beaten by Brazil.

CHARLIE WILLIAMS, later to attain fame as Britain's first black top rank comedian, transferred from Doncaster Rovers to Skegness Town, leading them to the championship of the Central Alliance League in 1961. (Charlie died in 2006, aged 77.)

INDUSTRIAL ESTATE, off Wainfleet Road, opened in October, the first unit being Heath End Hosiery Co. Ltd. of Hinckley, manufacturing nylon stockings. The first road on the estate was named Heath Road in commemoration. (The building is now occupied by Top of the Pile Quality Carpets Ltd.)

1960	LONDON TO SKEGNESS WALK held in January with a £100 prize for the winner. Of the 30 starters, half retired in the first 25 miles. The sixteen-year-old winner covered the 140 miles in something over 34 hours, but there were allegations that he had received several 'lifts' on the way, but the result was allowed to stand. The race was not repeated.
	LINCOLN ROAD constructed, providing a direct route from Burgh Road to the town centre. The work was carried out by Skegness Council in February.
	HIGH STREET AND PRINCE GEORGE STREET became one-way streets as from March 2.
	CLOCK TOWER ROUNDABOUT completed with raised wall topped by a grassed area, the scheme also including barrier walls along the adjacent footpaths and reconstruction of the dual carriageway in Lumley Road.
	SKEGNESS FLOWER LOVERS' CLUB formed in March.
	ST. CLEMENT'S CHURCH HALL opened near the old parish church of St. Clement's.
	SKEGNESS LIFEBOAT GUILD formed with the object of raising funds for the local lifeboat station. (April).
1961	MURPHY RADIO LTD., the first major manufacturing firm to set up in Skegness, moved from the Winter Gardens to a Council-built factory on the Wainfleet Road Industrial Estate with a labour force of nearly 500. (As Rank-Bush-Murphy, they closed down in the recession of 1975.)
	STIEBELS' nylon lace factory also opened a branch of their Nottingham works on the Industrial Estate.
	SKEGNESS PIER ANGLING CLUB formed and quickly enrolled more than a hundred members.
1962	HAYWOOD'S ROCK FACTORY, Cavendish Road, closed down. They were the first company to manufacture seaside rock in Skegness opening up in Rose Grove in 1920 before building the much bigger Cavendish Road factory, employing a large number of women.
	ENOCH POWELL, Minister of Health, made a visit of inspection to Skegness & District Hospital on July 21.

DUTTON'S CASH STORES, 43-45, Lumley Road, closed down. George H.J.Dutton, from Nottingham, had opened the shop in 1890, selling books and newspapers and other goods. It reopened soon afterwards as Lipton's supermarket, moving their premises from across the road, but was demolished in the 1980s to make way for Etam, and Greenwood' Menswear.

1963   SKEGNESS COAT-OF-ARMS. A competition was held for a design to replace that of the Earl of Scarbrough which the town has for long used as its emblem, with the earl's permission. Three designs were reproduced in the Skegness Standard of 1 January 1964, but no further action was taken. The Garter King of Arms had ruled that the town's Jolly Fisherman could only be incorporated as a 'supporter' and he would have to have both feet on the ground!

GIBRALTAR POINT INFORMATION CENTRE at the Nature Reserve officially opened by Sir Peter Scott.

BEECHING PLAN published disclosing that most of the railway network in Lincolnshire was to be axed, including the branch line to Skegness. In April, Skegness Council called a public meeting at the Embassy Centre and it was agreed to make a strong protest.

PIER HOTEL seriously damaged by a fire which started about 3 am on September 28 and a barman, aged 52, died on the top floor. The rebuilt structure was reduced in height with other alterations (The former hotel now trades as Barfly.)

FESTIVAL PAVILION roofed in, provided with heating and renamed the Festival Centre. (The building was finally demolished in 2001 and the site grassed over).

1964   BILLY BUTLIN served with writ by Skegness UD Council, owners of the Central Amusement Park, informing him that his tenancy would not be renewed and requiring vacation of the site. The ground was cleared at the end of the summer, greatly assisted when Mr. Butlin invited members of the public to a 'help yourself' exercise. Scores of people arrived on the Saturday morning, armed with saws, and hammers and other tools and set about knocking down the flimsy buildings and loading their vehicles with timber, hardboard sheets, pegboarding and other useful bits and pieces. At the end of the day the site was almost clear.

NEW TOWN HALL, North Parade, officially opened on July 9 by HRH the Princess Royal, supported by Skegness Council chairman, Cllr. Arthur Wise, JP., and other members and officers of the Council. The building was previously the NDFS Convalescent Home, opened in 1927.

SKEGNESS NEWS, edited by F.S.W.Major, closed down. Inaugurated in 1909 by Charles H. Major, Stanley's father, the News had followed Skegness's first newspaper, the Skegness Herald, after it was taken over by Charles Major.

PENSIONERS' HALL, Grantham Drive, opened in September by the Skegness OAP Association, providing greater accommodation and better facilities than the old building vacated in Alexandra Road. The cost was about £6,000

WHALE. A dead whale, 20 ft. long, washed up on the central beach in November was disposed of by waste merchants, Wing & Co. of Boston.

LIFEBOAT STATION received its first inflatable inshore lifeboat in May.

WATER SUPPLY transferred from Skegness UDC to the new East Lincolnshire Water Board whose area office occupied the whole of the second floor of the new Skegness Town Hall.

1965   SKEGNESS NATURELAND opened on July 1 by Skegness UD Council, with curator-manager John Yeadon and part-time technical director George Cansdale, television's Zoo Man.

BOTTON BROS. of Lowestoft, took over the Central Amusement Park, previously occupied by Butlin's, with an entire rebuild.

JOLLY FISHERMAN POSTER. John Hassall's original painting, commissioned by the Great Northern Railway in 1908, formally presented to Skegness Urban District Council by British Railways, along with the copyright. The painting had been hanging in the Council Chamber for a number of years, on loan from the railway. The handing-over ceremony took place at the Town Hall at the monthly Council Meeting when the painting and the deed of copyright were handed to chairman, Cllr. F.A.Wise, by Mr.P.M.Wright, divisional manager of Eastern Region, British Rail. (Skegness Standard, 3 March 1965.)

SKEGNESS & DISTRICT OPERATIC SOCIETY revived - after closure in the late 1930s - and produced 'The King and I' the same year.

1966   RAILWAY GOODS YARD at Skegness Station closed on May 2.

NOTTINGHAMSHIRE POOR GIRLS' HOLIDAY HOME, Brunswick Drive, closed down on retirement of matron Miss Gwendoline Cockerham who had been in charge since 1945. The building was later absorbed in the adjacent County Infants School.

BOSTON CREMATORIUM opened, the nearest to Skegness.

1967	SPRAT SHOAL. For about ten days, at the end of January and early February, a shoal of sprats, between the pier and Seaview Esplanade, attracted a host of fishing boats from Boston and other ports who trawled backwards and forwards, close to the shore. The sea was quite calm, but one heavily loaded boat sank going back across the Wash, the two crewmen being rescued by another boat.
	SEA SCOUTS, Skegness's first, formed under Group Scoutmaster Roland Broughton who was also secretary of Skegness Lifeboat Station.
1968	TELEPHONE EXCHANGE moved from the General Post Office, Roman Bank, to the other side of Lincoln Road, in a newly constructed building, opening on May 16.
	PRINCESS MARGARET visited Skegness on May 28, inspecting the St. John's Ambulance Brigade and Girl Guides and calling at Natureland and the Town Hall before attending a Youth Conference at Butlin's Holiday Camp.
	TED DWYER had his last summer on the Pier with his 'Follies on Parade' which had begun in 1950, a run of nineteen seasons.
	HOVERBOAT RIDES in a aircushion craft travelling at 40 mph were organised by Arthur Foreman and his son, Martin. The five mile trip cost 7s.6d. (38p) but lasted only the one summer because there was no protection for passengers soaked by the spray.
1969	SEWERAGE. Ingoldmells sewerage works completed by Spilsby Rural District Council with a marine pipeline discharging treated sewage effluent one and a half miles out to sea. The sea disposal scheme caused strong protest in Skegness and a petition was presented, without effect. (After the 1974 local government reorganisation, sewage disposal was taken over by Anglian Water Authority who closed down Skegness's Middlemarsh sewage disposal plant and directed Skegness sewage through the Ingoldmells works.)
	SKEGNESS HISTORICAL ASSOCIATION. At an invitation meeting at the Morris Secondary School a local branch of the Historical Association was formed with Rev. Clifford Clubley, vicar of Chapel St. Leonards, as chairman. A motion to form a Skegness History Society was defeated.
	SKEGNESS BOATING CLUB formed, primarily to help solve the problem of launching and recovering boats from the beach. A boat compound was constructed near the sands, SE of the Princes Parade car park, with one motor tractor. Membership increased rapidly and soon the compound held about a hundred small boats, employing three tractors.

1970 RAILWAY CLOSURE. Firsby Junction closed on October 5 together with all the East Lincolnshire line northward to Louth and Grimsby. The last train, a farewell excursion from Grimsby to London, ran on October 3, two days before the official closure date. The closures were all part of the hotly contested Beeching plan.

FIGURE 8 SWITCHBACK RAILWAY, North Parade, dismantled in March. It had been erected in 1908, owned by Thompson's Patent Gravity Switchback Railway Co. Ltd.

1971 DECIMAL DAY came to Britain on February 15, when halfcrowns, tanners and thruppenny-bits disappeared from the currency and both customers and shopkeepers fumbled with the coppers, undecided whether to call them 'pees' or 'newpence.' Television comedians had a field day, one relating how he asked an Irish barman if his till had been converted and he replied, 'No, sir, we're still Protestant.'

PIER ENTRANCE reconstructed for the second time, with removal of the central steps and side ramps. The £100,000 scheme incorporated a new amusement arcade and variety bar, and the main entrance was at ground level.

FORESHORE CENTRE. Tower Esplanade, demolished in January and a small Information Office was built on part of the site.

PRINCE OF WALES paid a private visit to the Gibraltar Point Nature Reserve where officials of the Lincolnshire Trust for Nature Conservation conducted him along one of the nature trails. (July.)

1972 BUTLIN HOUSE, Grand Parade, formerly headquarter offices of the Butlin organisation, demolished in January, with new shops and restaurant built on the site. It had been built in the late 1870s as the Osbert House Hotel at the south end of Frederica Terrace.

ARCADIA CENTRE, replacing Arcadia Theatre, after major reconstruction, officially opened on December 13 by the Rt.Hon. Viscount Eccles, minister responsible for the arts. The new centre, owned by East Lincolnshire Arts Centre Ltd., was to be operated by a local council of management.

POSTCODES introduced across Britain in May. Skegness and Boston postal codes were to be PE, indicating the Peterborough postal sorting office.

1973 FIRE STATION transferred from Roman Bank to new quarters off Burgh Road, adjacent to the waterworks, later named Churchill Avenue.

SKEGNESS BADMINTON CLUB formed.

WASH SWIM. The Wash was swum from Skegness to Hunstanton for the first time on May 26 by Sutton-in-Ashfield journalist, Kevin Murphy, in 13h.54m. He had previously conquered the English Channel in both directions and also the Irish Sea.

HISTORY CONFERENCE. The annual conference of the Historical Association of Great Britain was held at Skegness on April 14/16 arranged by the Skegness branch of the organisation.

1974 LOCAL GOVERNMENT REORGANISATION. Under new government legislation, Skegness Urban District Council ceased to exist after March 31. From April 1, Skegness became part of the new East Lindsey District Council. Different departments of the organisation were temporarily located at Skegness, Spilsby and Louth until purchase of the former Manby RAF College, near Louth, when they were centralised at the new headquarters known as Tedder Hall, Manby Park. A sub-office, for the use of local taxpayers was opened at Skegness Town Hall and in other towns. Skegness Town Council was also formed, but with limited power and resources. Lincolnshire County Council replaced the three former County Councils of Lindsey, Holland and Kesteven, but the northern part of the county, including Grimsby and Scunthorpe, was lost to the new Humberside County Council.

GIBRALTAR POINT Visitor Centre opened by Sir David Attenborough, after reconstruction of the existing buildings.

KING GEORGE V WALK, leading from Burgh Road to Winthorpe officially opened by Skegness's newly appointed first mayor, Cllr. Harold Fainlight, who had initiated the development. More than a thousand trees were planted and the walk was extended towards Church Lane in 1989 when Cllr. Fainlight was again mayor. Mr. Alan Birks was in charge of the administrative arrangements.

POLICE HQ. Lincolnshire Police Divisional Headquarters and Courthouse, Park Avenue, officially opened on March 18 by Sir Arthur Peterson, KCB, MVO, permanent under-secretary of state to the Home Office. The previous Skegness police station and courthouse had been on Roman Bank, at the Ida Road junction.

SKEGNESS PROBUS CLUB established, the first lunch being held at the Imperial Cafe, presided over by president Reg Davey.

FIRE AT BUTLIN'S CAMP. During the afternoon of June 5 a fire broke out in a large steel-framed glass and concrete building containing a restaurant, coffee bar and amusement arcade. It was quickly evacuated and fire brigades from a.-wide~area were soon in attendance, the flames being visible ten miles away. The building was completely gutted and the cause was said to be an electrical fault.

TELEVISION. With other parts of Lincolnshire, Skegness was transferred from ITV's Anglia region to Yorkshire, beamed from the Belmont mast, on the Lincolnshire Wolds.

1975 SKEGNESS POTTERY opened in part of Pountney's Garage, Burgh Road by John Pountney and during the summer it was said to have welcomed fifty thousand visitors. When the garage business closed down the pottery took over the whole building and established a cafe as well as opening branches in Lumley Road and at Boston and Lincoln. The large garage had been established by John's father, Frank Pountney, in the early 1920s with a Ford sole agency for the whole of the Skegness area. (The premises are now mainly occupied by Jackson Building Centres Ltd.)

1976 RICHMOND COUNTY PRIMARY SCHOOL, Richmond Drive, opened by Lincolnshire County Council on the site of the pre-war Skegness United Football Ground.

BERRY WAY, one-way link road between Wainfleet Road, Lincoln Road and Roman Bank, opened for traffic. Named after W.H.Berry who brought the first motor car to Skegness and opened the first garage and town bus service. His business premises occupied ground near the new road.

SKEGNESS LIONS CLUB formed in June, with Barry Sturgess president.

PARADE CINEMA building reopened as the Penny Parade amusement arcade, owned by Joe Sales. The application for change of use was refused by the Council, but granted on appeal.

CHURCH FARM MUSEUM, Church Road, officially opened on May 19 by Councillor Harold Fainlight who had played a big part in its inception. The museum was formed from a collection of farm implements and machines displayed by Bernard Best at The Grange, Bratoft. After he died his widow gave the collection to Lincolnshire County Council and Councillor Fainlight persuaded them to put the items on show at Church Farm which the Council had purchased two years earlier. Further agricultural artefacts were added and the farmhouse refurnished with objects from those earlier days.

1977 RED HOUSE HOTEL, Scarbrough Avenue, demolished in May, after standing derelict since destruction by wartime bombing. Residential flats were afterwards built on the site at the junction with Park Avenue.

SIR WILLIAM BUTLIN VISITED Skegness for the last time when he was invited to switch on the foreshore illuminations. He stayed at the County Hotel, North Parade, built on the site of his first Skegness amusement park.

1978	PIER DESTRUCTION. On the night of January 11, a northerly gale combined with a spring tide to tear two huge gaps in the pier, each about 50 yards wide, leaving the pierhead and the shelters as two islands.

The storm also smashed down the south end of Lagoon Walk and seriously eroded the dunes further south. More damage was sustained with the waves biting into the dunes fronting the North Shore golf links for about twenty yards. In Ingoldmells a part of the sea wall was washed down and caravan sites flooded.

BUS STATION, Drummond Road - opened in 1937 by the Lincolnshire Road Car Company - closed on May 14. The station was moved to Richmond Drive, next to the railway station, which had been used as a bus station carrying passengers to and from Butlins holiday camp after arrival by train.

SKEGNESS & WINTHORPE PAROCHIAL COUNCIL formed. A year before, Skegness rector, Rev. Roderick Wells, had been appointed priest-in-charge of St.Mary's, Winthorpe, after the last Winthorpe vicar resigned in 1976.

TOWER CINEMA changed ownership and extensive alterations resulted in the cinema being moved to a new upper floor and the ground floor reserved for amusements.

1979	ROMAN BANK METHODIST CHURCH closed on Sunday morning, September 23, and the service was followed by the congregation walking in procession to the Algitha Road Methodist Church where a communion service was held uniting the two congregations.

SNOWFALL in February said to be the heaviest for a number of years.

TOWN TWINNING. Skegness Twinning Association formed to twin with Bad Gandersheim in Germany.

SKEGNESS CAST STONE WORKS Ltd. closed down in February. Founded in the early 1920s by local builder, Henry Lill, for the manufacture of pre-cast concrete products the business was continued by his sons, Philip and Douglas and grandson, Robin. The site had earlier accommodated the Wainfleet Road brickworks.

1980	SEELY HOUSE CONVALESCENT HOME, Roman Bank, Seathorne, demolished after being closed as a National Health Service home in 1978. It had been established in 1891 as a result of a legacy left by Sir Charles Seely, Nottingham MP, and later became the Nottinghamshire Miners Convalescent Home before being taken over by the National Health Service.

YMCA HOLIDAY CAMP for children and the mentally handicapped, situated on the north side of Royal Oak Terrace, Roman Bank, closed-down after about forty years' use. (The building was gutted by fire in December 1981.)

SKEGNESS CRICKET GROUND centenary celebrated with a dinner and centenary cricket match featuring a number of well-known county players (September).

ST. MATTHEW'S CHURCH HALL, Ida Road, sold by auction in September. The Parochial Church Council stated that expensive repairs were required and the money was needed for church improvements.

GRANDWAYS SUPERMARKET opened at Old Wainfleet Road on May 13.

LAGOON WALK further damaged by October storm, collapsing for a distance of 50 yards.

SIR WILLIAM BUTLIN died on June 12, aged 81, and was buried in Jersey, his retirement home with an impressive headstone commemorating his life and achievements.

1981   MAGISTRATES' COURT. With the closure of Spilsby Sessions House, as from January 1, courts were arranged to take place in Skegness Courthouse every Monday.

SKEGNESS STANDARD printed as a tabloid as from January 30. The price remained at 15p.

CRICKET GROUND. Thirteen large trees bordering the ground felled because of Dutch elm disease, in April. The remainder were cut down before the end of the year.

WATER TOWER at Burgh Road Waterworks demolished in June. It had been built by Skegness UDC in 1927 but had become redundant.

SKEGNESS & DISTRICT HOSPITAL maternity unit closed on June 30, the last baby (Barry Lee Robinson) being born at 7.30 am that day. The unit had opened in 1939.

1982   WOODSIDE HOLIDAY CENTRE, Grosvenor Road, belonging to the YMCA, closed down at the end of the summer. It had been founded by the YMCA as a tented holiday camp for ex-servicemen in 1921.

NEW COASTGUARD STATION, at the sea end of Winthorpe Avenue, officially opened in May by the town mayor, Cllr. Ken Holland. The tower, 55 ft. high, was the last contract carried out by old established local builders, William Greetham & Son, at a cost of £125,000.

WRATES' PHOTOGRAPHY, Lumley Road, went into voluntary liquidation and closed in December. The family firm was founded in 1907 and for many summers their popular 'walking snaps' were a feature on the seafronts at Skegness and Mablethorpe.

EMBASSY BALLROOM converted to the multi-purpose Embassy Centre in a million pound makeover, commencing in January and completed near the end of December. The new layout included an auditorium seating 1,200 people, the lower area of 760 seats capable of being cleared for exhibitions and other activities, as well as use as a theatre.

THE JUNGLE. The last of the undeveloped ground, fronting North Parade, Castleton Boulevard and Park Avenue, cleared of trees in preparation for the erection of houses and residential flats. A public petition for preservation of the Boulevard frontage had been rejected by the Council.

CAMELS from Longleat provided rides on Lagoon Walk for the second and last summer season.

1983   LION HOTEL'S Lumley Road frontage converted to a shopping arcade.

HORNCASTLE PARLIAMENTARY DIVISION. Horncastle Division Conservative Association held their last meeting in Alford on April 6, followed by the inaugural meeting of the new East Lindsey Constituency Association. The sitting (Conservative) member for the Horncastle Division, Mr. Peter Tapsell, was adopted for the new East Lindsey Parliamentary Division. The Horncastle Division, which had included Skegness, had been formed in 1885. The revision also resulted in the formation of the Boston and Skegness Parliamentary Division.

BURGH ROAD BRICKWORKS chimney demolished. In its later years the brickworks was owned by Skegness Brick & Tile Company, a subsidiary of William Greetham & Son, an old established local building contractor, and stood at the junction of Old Burgh Road and Beacon Way.

RAILWAY STATION BUFFET closed down.

MIDDLEMARSH SEWERAGE WORKS, Burgh Marsh, advertised for sale by Anglian Water Authority. The works was established by Skegness UD Council in 1933 and ceased operating when Anglian Water took over after the 1974 local government reorganisation as they switched to the installation at Ingoldmells.

PANTON PORK BUTCHERS, 47, Lumley Road, closed down on Christmas Eve. Fred Panton established the business in High Street in 1921 before moving to 83, Lumley Road. He sold the premises to the Co-op. in 1946 to become part of their new department store and moved up to No.47. It was a very popular shop, carried on by his family after he died.

1984	SCOOTER RALLY on Sat.-Sun., October 6-7, on South Bracing car park and the Festival Centre, caused enormous damage and widespread drunkenness and disorderly behaviour. The South Bracing beach chalets were totally destroyed, wrecked for firewood, by the rampaging visitors.
	ARCADIA CENTRE, Drummond Road, closed in October. Taken over by East Lincolnshire Arts in 1972, it had operated as a theatre and arts centre, but two poor seasons ran it into debt. The building was demolished in 1988 and the site was converted to a car park
	GIBRALTAR POINT designated a National Nature Reserve.
	G.J.CROFTS STORES in Lumley Road which had opened in 1880 and closed in 1983, demolished to form three new shops, occupied by Nationwide, Dixon's Electrical and Baker's Oven. Founder, G.J.Crofts, had died in 1923, but the business was continued by his family.
1985	THE HALL, Roman Bank, advertised for sale by Strutt & Parker's Grantham branch with 'offers in the region of £220,000.' The freehold site of 2.1 acres included the early l9th. century residence, coach-house and stables, all said to be in a poor state because of long non-occupation. No mention of the round brick dovecote in the grounds, also in a state of decay.
	PIER DEMOLITION. After the fatal storm of 1978, the section carrying the shelters was dismantled in 1984 and the demolition and removal of the pierhead was effected this year. On Saturday evening, October 28, workmen left an incinerator unattended and a spark ignited nearby woodwork to set the whole structure ablaze. The blackened steelwork was afterwards dismantled by contractors working between tides.
	ST. CLEMENT'S CEMETERY declared closed with further burials continued at St. Mary's, Winthorpe.
	DAY CENTRE for the elderly and infirm officially opened at Skegness Hospital by the Earl of Scarbrough on July 8.
	SKEGNESS 2000, a town pressure group, formed on October 1 at a meeting at the County Hotel. (It later became Skegness Town Forum, and eventually Skegness Civic Society.)
	DEAD SPERM WHALE washed ashore in early March between end of Seacroft Golf links and Gibraltar Point. Buried near the dunes on March 5 in grave excavated by Rawlinson's two bulldozers.
	SKEGNESS NEWS revived on October 3 by Morton's of Horncastle, with editorial office at 46, Algitha Road.

1986	CLOCK TOWER clock electrified, eliminating the weekly manual winding.

EARL OF SCARBROUGH HIGH SCHOOL Burgh Road, opened in September, incorporating the Morris Secondary School and replacing the Lumley Secondary School in Pelham Road. The new building fronting Burgh Road was not completed until 1988.

PANDA'S PALACE children's play centre, off Tower Esplanade, opened on May 23.

LAWN COACH PARK sold by East Lindsey District Council to Summerbridge Properties Ltd. for £1,225,000 for redevelopment as a Grandways supermarket, the coach station being transferred to Richmond Drive.

SHADES HOTEL, Lumley Road, reopened on May 23 after major alterations and extension to Samuels' former shop next door, as well as a second frontage in High Street. The previous major alterations were in 1935 when the roof was raised to form an upstairs lounge. (In 2006, after further extensive alterations, the Shades name gave way to the Variety Bar.)

1987	LUMLEY HOTEL Long Bar demolished. The single storey building was set at right angles to the hotel with a large clock above the central entrance, to remind train travellers they just had time for a quick one! (The area is now occupied by Iceland Supermarket.)

HILDREDS HOTEL, High Street, demolished in April to make way for the Hildreds shopping centre

TELEPHONE EXCHANGE, Lincoln Road, closed on Feb. 20 and Skegness and Spilsby telephone lines were switched to Grantham for automatic operation. The telephone linesmen continued to occupy part of the building.

SEACROFT FIELDS housing development, south of Richmond Drive, commenced building with plans for over 400 new houses.

LAGOON WALK collapsed at the southern end on Dec. 6 after the morning tide undermined the steel piling.

GRAVESTONE RECORDING carried out in St. Clement's cemetery by a team organised by East Lincolnshire Community Programme. Gravestone inscriptions were recorded and located on a plan for identification and copies were deposited at the Lincolnshire Archives Office, the Society of Geneologists in London and with the local clergy.

RAY CLEMENCE, Skegness-born international goalkeeper who attended the former Lumley Secondary School, awarded an MBE. The 38 year old ex-Liverpool and Tottenham Hotspur keeper was capped 61 times for England and later became goalkeeping coach for the England team.

1988	HMS ROYAL ARTHUR ASSOCIATION formed by ex-naval personnel who had trained at Butlin's Skegness Holiday Camp during the Second World War. Subsequently an annual gathering lasting several days was held in Skegness-Ingoldmells with parades, church services and social events. (The Association held their final meeting in 2006 when the Bishop of Lincoln preached in Ingoldmells parish church and the Skegness street procession was led by HM Royal Marines Band.)
	THE HILDREDS Shopping Centre officially opened by television celebrity Paul Daniels, on September 17, situated on land previously occupied by Hildreds Hotel and shops in High Street and Briar Way. Gateway Supermarket constituted the largest single unit.
	RICHMOND DRIVE COACH STATION completed, although part of it was in use the previous summer following the closure of the Lawn Motor Park.
	THE HALL, Roman Bank, demolished in March in preparation for building residential flats known as Sutton Court.
	ARCADIA CENTRE, Drummond Road, demolished March-April. (The area became a Council car park in 1993.)
	ROSE BEARINGS engineering works at Church Road South taken over by Minebea of Tokyo, a world class manufacturer of steel bearings and other products.
	FLASH FLOOD on July 4 with three inches of rain falling between 5 and 7 pm. Houses, shops and other buildings in many parts of the town suffered serious flooding and damage.
	EARL OF SCARBROUGH SPORTS CENTRE at the High School officially opened by the Earl of Scarbrough.
	SKEGNESS ALPHA CLUB formed from members of the disbanded Skegness Business & Professional Women's Club.
1989	ANSTRUTHER HOUSE, Drummond Road, demolished. In the early part of the century it had been the home and surgery of Dr. Alexander Allan, father of film star, Elizabeth Allan (1908-90). The building stood at the south end of the present Arcadia Car Park, opened shortly afterwards
	INDOOR SWIMMING POOL opened, adjoining the open-air pool at the rear of the Embassy Centre, on May 20.
	SKEGNESS INTERNAL DRAINAGE BOARD amalgamated with the Alford and Louth Boards, with offices at Manby Park.
	DERBYSHIRE MINERS' HOLIDAY CENTRE, Winthorpe Avenue, sold to Rinkfield Leisure in August. It continued for a time as the Sands Holiday Village but was then converted to a luxury caravan site.

SKEGNESS GRAMMAR SCHOOL became the first grant maintained school in the country under new Thatcher legislation. Education Secretary Kenneth Clark gave it official approval in February, the minister himself later visiting the school.

SEAGULL formed at a meeting at the Crown Hotel in March with the object of promoting green issues and protecting the environment. Mrs Julie Crowson became chairman.

JOLLY FISHERMAN STATUE. Sculptor Ross Walker commissioned by town mayor, Cllr. Harold Fainlight, MBE, JP, and other subscribers to produce a representation of Hassall's famous character. The completed statue was displayed on a circular plinth in the Compass Gardens and officially unveiled in May. Shortly afterwards, a more pedestrian version, by an unknown sculptor, was placed in the railway station.

NATURELAND SEAL HOSPITAL opened and received its first patient in June.

GOLF. Skegness golfer, Miss Helen Dobson, won the British Women's Amateur Championship and also became the first golfer to hold the English Girls' and Ladies' British titles at the same time. Helen afterwards turned professional.

ROAD RUNNER BUSES. 'Hail and Ride' mini-buses, operated by Lincolnshire Road Car Co., began a town service in November.

SKATEBOARDING. A delegation of youngsters requested the Town Council to help in providing a skateboard rink. The Council donated £500 for the project and the rink was built on the Wainfleet Road Playing Fields, but was eventually dismantled after falling into disuse.

1990   INGOLDMELLS FORESHORE SOLD by the Parish Council to Sheffield leisure firm, Arnold Laver & Co. Ltd., for more than a million pounds. The sale included the beach, promenades, shops, chalets, car parks and caravan site owned by the Council. Under the Thatcher government's poll tax proposals, business rates from these properties would go to central government, imposing an unbearable burden on residents. The tax change never became law, but the sale enabled Ingoldmells to pay off its heavy loan debts and make other substantial savings. The reported sale price was £1,034,000 plus VAT.

NEW LIFEBOAT STATION, Tower Esplanade, officially opened on September 30 when the new lifeboat, 'The Lincolnshire Poacher', was also named and dedicated. The old lifeboathouse at South Parade was afterwards sold for commercial use.

HIGHEST TIDE for eighteen years, on Saturday night, October 6, brought about by 60 mph winds, reached up to the new lifeboat station and brought in hundreds of tons of sand.

BOOTS' CHEMISTS extended their Lumley Road premises to take in the shop next door, reopening on November 28.

CROWN HOTEL, Seacroft, reopened in September after major alterations and refurbishment by new owner, Skegness building contractor, Arthur Mason.

SUTTON COURT, Roman Bank,- opened on the site of the Old Hall, a residential development provided by Lincourt Retirement Homes with 56 one and two-bedroom units and warden service.

1991 WAINFLEET BY-PASS opened to traffic on Feb. 22. Work had commenced in Feb. 1990 and the improvement cost £3,250,000.

BUTLIN'S FUNCOAST WORLD, previously Butlin's Holiday Camp, completed multi-million pound redevelopment which had begun in 1986.

HOUSE REFUSE COLLECTION passed by East Lindsey District Council to private contractors as from October.

SEWERAGE. After numerous complaints of beach and sea pollution, as well as unpleasant smells emanating from the Ingoldmells sewage disposal works, local environment groups made strong protests about the effects on both human and marine life. It was alleged that at peak times crude sewage was being pumped into the sea.

SKEGNESS GRAMMAR SCHOOL took over Wainfleet Hall for boarders' accommodation.

1992 SAFEWAY SUPERMARKET, Wainfleet Road, opened on the site of the former railway goods yard on Sept. 15.

PRINCE EDWARD WALK, the two-tier concrete sea wall and marine walk between Seaview Esplanade and the pier, officially opened by HRH Prince Edward on Feb. 29. The prince afterwards attended other functions at Butlin's Funcoast World and the Richmond Leisure Centre.

RECTOR. In September the Rev. G.J.Wickstead was appointed to take charge of Skegness and Winthorpe churches, succeeding the Rev. Ernest Adley who had left the previous October. Under a diocese ruling issued in 1991, no more rectors are to be appointed in the diocese and the Rev. Wickstead was designated priest-in-charge.

RAMBLERS' ASSOCIATION, SKEGNESS GROUP. After the Rev. Norman Walker called a public meeting at the Baptist Hall in September 1991, the first Annual General Meeting was held at the same venue on 14 April with about forty people present. Frank Skelton was elected chairman and Frank Smith secretary, also a committee and other officers. A constitution was adopted and a programme of events approved.

1993   CAREY HOUSE CONVALESCENT HOME, Roman Bank, Seathorne, demolished in December. It had been a convalescent home for women under the National Health Service after opening in the 1930s as the Nottinghamshire Women's Convalescent Home.

POST OFFICE, Roman Bank, closed down and the service moved to the Co-op. stores in Lumley Road on February 24.

MINIATURE RAILWAY, running between Tower Esplanade and Princes Parade, closed in January. Malcolm Stuart, who had operated it for thirteen years, refused to accept a further short-term lease.

ICELAND SUPERMARKET, Lumley Square, opened in April, built on the site of the Lumley Hotel's Long Bar.

LUMLEY SECONDARY SCHOOL, Pelham Road ,demolished to make room for a new County Junior School. The Lumley School had opened in 1932.

HRH DUCHESS OF GLOUCESTER arrived in a helicopter on the Wainfleet Road Playing Fields on Sept. 30 to unveil a plaque commemorating the opening of the new Sea Scouts Hall. She then went on to perform a similar service at the Derbyshire Children's Holiday Home in Scarbrough Avenue, marking a £250,000 extension and modernisation improvement, and finally went on to Friskney to open newly built charity bungalows.

CITIZENS ADVICE BUREAU opened in Drummond Road on Feb. 20.

KWIK-SAVE SUPERMARKET took over Grandways at Church Road South on Feb 22.

1994   SALVATION ARMY CITADEL, High Street demolished in October, to be replaced by a new Church. The old building had opened in 1929.

BEACH NOURISHMENT to raise the level of the beaches commenced at Ingoldmells Point in mid-April. In the next four years the National Rivers Authority planned to pump millions of tonnes of sand from the seabed of the Wash onto beaches stretching northward to Mablethorpe.

SUNDAY TRADING regulations relaxed to allow opening of supermarkets and other traders for seven days a week, with effect from August 26. (Sunday Trading Act, 1994.)

SKEGNESS FORUM formed at a meeting at the Embassy Centre on February 24, replacing the former Skegness 2000. Mr. Harold Fainlight, MBE, JP., was appointed chairman, with Councillor Mark Anderson vice-chairman. Mr. John King became secretary and treasurer. The new organisation involved a wide range of local commercial and charitable bodies.

1995   SKEGNESS COUNTY JUNIOR SCHOOL built on site of the demolished Lumley Secondary School at a cost of £1.1m. The new school contained twelve classrooms and opened on January 18, the entrance being from Pelham Road.

NEW SALVATION ARMY CITADEL in High Street opened on November 1, on ground next to the replaced church.

SKEGNESS & DISTRICT COMBINED EX-SERVICES ASSOCIATION formed on March 9 with membership open to the Royal British Legion and other nominated armed forces organisations. The association was formed to celebrate the fiftieth anniversary of VE Day (8 May 1945) and VJ Day (14 August 1945).

1996   CLOCK TOWER RESTORATION carried out at a cost of £70,000 and reopened in May. The clock mechanism was repaired and brickwork and masonry as well as the four clock faces. The tower was shrouded in polythene sheeting round the scaffolding throughout the winter and spring.

COMPASS GARDENS, Tower Esplanade and North Bracing entirely reconstructed, with the Jolly Fisherman statue incorporated in a water feature. The last item was not an initial success and costly alterations were necessary to get it working properly.

HIGH STREET RECONSTRUCTION, with coloured paving, completed and opened with restricted hours for motor traffic extending from May to September.

STONE LION, which had stood on the pavement on the Roman Bank frontage of the Lion Hotel for over ninety years, removed by landlord shortly before the hotel was sold to Wetherspoon. When the new owners took over they renamed the old-established hotel the Red Lion.

FREEMAN, HARDY & WILLIS shoe shop, 56, Lumley Road, closed down after trading there for most of the century. The premises were later taken over by Specsavers.

ARGOS CATALOGUE SHOP opened on the former Lumley Road frontage of the Lion Hotel with extensions at the rear (October).

COURTHOUSE EXTENSION, Park Avenue, opened on October 19 by Lord Lieutenant of Lincolnshire, Mrs. Bridget Cracroft-Eley, JP.

NORTH SHORE SEA WALL. R.G.Mitchell's North Shore Golf Club erected notices in February on the North Shore pullover stating that the new sea defence wall was built on private land and there was no public footpath across it although access was not restricted.

OLD GAS SHOWROOMS, Lumley Square, which had stood empty for some time, reopened by Kentucky Fried Chicken (KFC).

1997   BURGH-SKEGNESS CYCLEWAY officially opened on March 26, commemorating Richard Holmes of Burgh who died tragically in a motor cycle accident two years earlier.

METHODIST CHURCH CIRCUIT of Skegness and Wainfleet combined with the Alford circuit to form the Alford, Skegness and Wainfleet Circuit. The new amalgamation took in 22 places of worship, four ministers and 43 local preachers and worship leaders. The meeting was held at Algitha Road church on September 5 and the superintendent minister of the new circuit was to be Rev.A.M.Barker, residing in Alford, with the Rev.J.G. Graham continuing as the Skegness minister.

DEAD SPERM WHALE washed up near pier, drifting to Lagoon Walk on December 3. The following day, bulldozers dragged it onto Tower Esplanade where it was loaded onto a low-platform vehicle and transported to a special landfill site at Winterton, near Scunthorpe. The whale was 35 ft. long, weighing about 40 tonnes, and it had a large wound on its back..

RIALTO BRIDGE on the south boating lake was replaced by one giving better access to the large island.

SKEGNESS PLAYGOERS SOCIETY held a festival of play readings at the Embassy Theatre, 50 years after their 1947 revival following wartime suspension. The readings were spread over a period of three weeks in May-June.

1998   MAJOR'S BOOKSHOP, 41, Lumley Road, closed down on January 17 after more than a hundred years trading in the same premises (C.H.Major & Co.Ltd.). After extensive alterations the building was reopened by Edinburgh Woollen Mill on August 15.

BUTLIN'S GAIETY THEATRE at Funcoast World holiday centre demolished as part of the multi-million pound redevelopment. The theatre had stood for sixty years, during which many of Britain's brightest stars

1998 from the world of entertainment had trod its boards. The building began life at the 1932 British Empire Exhibition in Glasgow as a very temporary theatre, actually for only a month whilst the exhibition lasted. When it closed, Billy Butlin bought the steel-framed structure at a bargain price, moved it to Skegness and re-erected it as the camp theatre. The war came along before it could be opened and the Royal Navy used it to project films for training purposes. When peace came it began a new life as the Gaiety, seating an audience of two thousand campers.

INDUSTRIAL ESTATE, Wainfleet Road, extended with 16 one acre plots in March.

SKEGNESS INFANT SCHOOL, Cavendish Road, demolished in February and the school moved into temporary accommodation until the replacement was completed. The new building, standing farther back from the road, was officially opened on May 21 by HRH the Duke of Gloucester. The duke also performed the opening ceremony of Wainfleet's refurbished market place on the same day.

DERBYSHIRE CHILDREN'S HOLIDAY CENTRE, Scarbrough Avenue, reopened on April 4 after closing in 1995. The reopening followed receipt of a £235,000 National Lottery Grant which secured its future for the next three years.

SAYERS' JEWELLERY shop at 39, Lumley Road, closed down on March 28 after trading for more than a hundred years.

GIBRALTAR POINT NATURE RESERVE celebrated its 50th. Anniversary in December. A new 'wetlands' area at Jackson's Marsh nearby was being excavated to add to the conservation land.

SKEGNESS JOLLY FISHERMAN POSTER. Town Clerk, Alan Crawshaw, reported to Town Council that the official documents relating to the copyright of the poster had now been recovered from East Lindsey District Council where they had been since 1974, although ELDC were unaware of it. Permission to reproduce the logo must now be obtained from the Town Council. (Skegness Standard, 3.4.98)

MARINE HOTEL, at the Lumley Road - Drummond Road junction, became the Marine Boathouse after purchase by Dean Gillison whose family had been running the business since 1967. The new owner carried out a comprehensive makeover with new entrance and balconies to high standards. Built as part of Gomersall Terrace in the early 1880s, it was converted to a hotel by W.B.Lambe soon after the Great War ended.

1999   BEACH CRIME. In January the brutal murder of a young local schoolboy took place near the Seaview Pullover and later in the year a man was convicted and sentenced to life imprisonment.

CCTV completed its first year operating in Skegness in June when it was reported that it had detected or deterred some 600 crimes.

EMBASSY THEATRE DEMOLISHED in November, to be reconstructed and modernised, whilst retaining the 1982 additions.

OUTDOOR SWIMMING POOL also filled in and the area prepared for conversion to car parking space.

LUMLEY ROAD ONE-WAY traffic plan, proposed by the county council, met fierce opposition and in November it was announced that the idea had been dropped.

JANICE SUTTON SCHOOL OF DANCE put on a show at the London Palladium in February when the young performers received a great reception.

2000   POLICE REORGANISATION. The three divisional centres, including Skegness, centralised at Lincoln for emergency calls with a new digital communications office.

SKEGNESS DRAINAGE BOARD amalgamated with Alford and Louth to form Lindsey Marsh Drainage Board. Founded in the 1930s, the three boards had already shared the same facilities at Manby Park for several years.

SKEGNESS SOCIETY. At a meeting at the Crown Hotel on May 15, under chairman Mr. Harold Fainlight, MBE., it was agreed to replace the Skegness Forum with the Skegness Society and a new constitution was adopted. Mr. Eric Haywood was appointed secretary and treasurer and it was decided to register the Society with the Civic Trust. (The Society was incorporated as Skegness Civic Society Ltd. in 2003.)

TOURISM INFORMATION CENTRE transferred in May from the Embassy Centre to a new building across the road at the entrance to Tower Gardens.

NEW OPEN AIR SWIMMING POOL opened on Saturday, July 1, on the south side of the Embassy Centre.

GREAT GALE on Sunday-Monday, October 30-31, blew down the main stand on Skegness Town football ground at Burgh Road, overturned caravans and uprooted several street trees. In Yorkshire, Kent and other areas it was followed by serious river flooding.

2000   SKEGNESS MILLENNIUM FIRST COLLEGE, Heath Road, officially opened on November 17. The £4m college, a partnership between East Lindsey District Council and East Lindsey ITEC, offers training in catering, computers, management, health, childcare and other subjects.

POST OFFICE moved from the Lumley Road Co-op. department stores to their new foodstore in the Hildreds shopping mall on Monday, November 26.

LIDL SUPERMARKET opened in Richmond Drive, next to the bus station, November 30. The German company was stated to have 4,000 shops across Europe.

TRAVELLER TROUBLE. Large numbers of 'travellers' in cars and trailers descended on Skegness on December 23, packing the Embassy Theatre and Scarbrough Esplanade car parks. The unwelcome visitors forced pubs to close because of their disorderly behaviour and some damage was caused. Police moved them to the Festival Centre car park on December 27 and they finally departed on January 2. The Janice Sutton show at the Embassy Theatre had to be cancelled and the New Year street celebrations postponed. Cleaning up the filth and rubbish of the occupation cost the taxpayers thousands of pounds and there was much criticism because the authorities were unable to find legal means of dispersing them sooner.

BEACON MEDICAL PRACTICE removed from Algitha Road to town outskirts in a purpose-built building at Churchill Avenue. (April.)

TOWE GARDENS officially reopened on July 2 by Cllr. M. Clark, Chairman of ELDC, after an attractive makeover greatly assisted by the Town and District councillor.

CO-OP. FOODSTORE removed from Lumley Road to former Somerfield supermarket in The Hildreds in April. In November, the Post Office had also relocated from the Lumley Road CO-op. to join the Hildreds Co-operative there.

The famous 'Jolly Fisherman' poster with its 'so bracing' slogan was painted by John Hassall (1868-1948) for the Great Northern Railway Company in 1908. The artist was paid the princely sum of £12 for the picture that was to make Skegness known nationwide and even farther afield.

(Below.) John Hassall (right) receiving an illuminated address from Councillor Fred Cooper, chairman of Skegness U.D. Council on 9 June 1936, the only known occasion he visited the town. Also in the picture are Councillor Joseph Crawshaw (left), Arthur Barlow (secretary of Skegness Advancement Association) and Councillor Frank Wood. The original painting is shown, here on the wall of the Council Chamber at the earlier Town Hall on Roman Bank.

POPULATION OF SKEGNESS AND WINTHORPE.
1801-2001.

Year	Skegness	Winthorpe.	Year	Skegness	Winthorpe.
1801	134	221	1901	2,140	379
1811	132	174	1911	3,775	511
1821	150	233	1921	9,246* (5,550)	698
1831	185	244	1931	9,122	-
1841	316	273	1941	-	-
1851	366	299	1951	12,539	-
1861	322	305	1961	12,847	-
1871	349	285	1971	13,580	-
1881	1,332	337	1981	14,590	-
1891	1,488	326	1991	16,355	-
			2001	18,910	-

The figures for 1901-91 were compiled from information supplied by the Office for National Statistics and Crown copyright material is reproduced with the permission of Her Majesty's Stationery Office. The figure for the 2001 census is reproduced under the terms of the Click-Use Licence (No. C 2006010182) by permission of HMSO. Earlier data is taken from the Victoria County History: Lincolnshire, vol.2 (1906).

Skegness was connected to the railway network in 1873 and in 1877 the Earl of Scarbrough began building the new town, which accounts for the increase of a thousand new residents during that decade.

* Although the parish of Winthorpe was incorporated in Skegness in 1926, the 1931 census showed a smaller population than ten years earlier. This was said to be accounted for by the fact that the 1921 count was taken on June 19 when a number of seasonal residents and visitors would be included. The 1931 census was taken two months earlier, on April 26, before the holiday season had begun. An unofficial amendment deducted 3,696 visitors from the census figure, to leave 5,550 residents in 1921.

Because of the Second World War, no census was taken in 1941.

SKEGNESS 1793

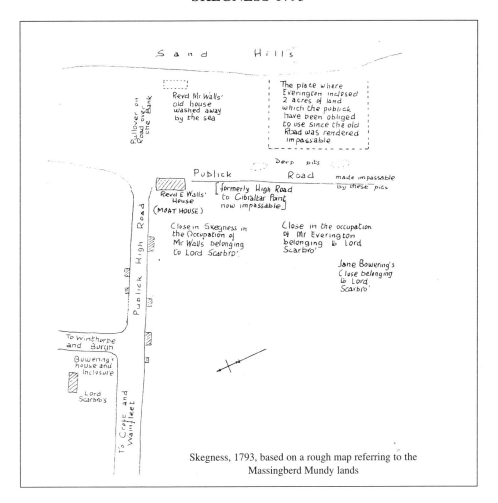

Skegness, 1793, based on a rough map referring to the Massingberd Mundy lands

Two hundred years ago, Skegness was no more than a one-street village leading to the sea, eventually to become the High Street. Roman Bank divided at the western end, one branch leading to Wainfleet and the other to Ingoldmells and Burgh-le-Marsh. The Rev. Edward Walls had built a house on the pullover which had been washed down and he then replaced it with a new building a little further inland, but still on the edge of the beach. Known as the Moat House, it became a high-class lodging house where the Tennysons and other local gentry stayed on their excursions to the coast. The road to Gibraltar Point at that date was in such poor state as to be unusable by vehicles. The population was about 130.

SKEGNESS 1849

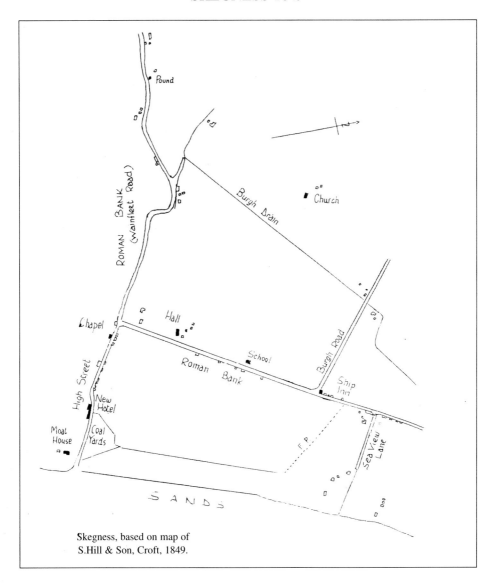

Skegness, based on map of
S.Hill & Son, Croft, 1849.

SKEGNESS, 1849.

The mid-19th. century found Skegness still a very small village, with about 350 residents, and the bordering parish of Winthorpe had another 300. The church of St. Clement's stood well inland, reached by rough roads and field paths after an earlier building had been destroyed by the sea. The New Hotel in the High Street was kept by landlord Joseph Hildred whose wife renamed it after him when he died. The other hotel was the Vine, well off the map, on the left, under landlord Thomas Enderby.

Colliers from Tyneside landed several thousand tons of coal on the sands every year and this was carted to a coal yard, shown on the map, now partly taken up by the Tower Gardens.

The Hall, on Roman Bank, belonged to the land-owning Earl of Scarbrough and the house, with grounds, was occupied by William Everington, the earl's largest tenant farmer. The building was demolished in 1988 to be replaced by Sutton Court housing development. The school, shown further along Roman Bank, opened in 1839, controlled by the established church and maintained by grants, donations and the weekly penny per week paid for each pupil.

The Ship Inn, at the Burgh Road junction, was quite new in 1849 and was actually just inside Winthorpe parish. It was demolished in 1936 and the present Ship was built just across the road on the newly-opened Castleton Boulevard. Burgh Drain, later piped in, was then a wide open watercourse with an outfall into the sea at what is now North Shore Road.

The 'Pound,' marked on Wainfleet Road, was the local pinfold where stray cattle, sheep and horses were impounded and fees demanded before their release. The bend and curve,to the right of Wainfleet Road, is now Old Wainfleet Road, the highway being straightened out in the early 1930s.

The Earl of Scarbrough's town development plan of 1878, although it did not turn out quite like this. No marketplace was laid out between Algitha and Ida Roads and two streets planned between Scarbrough Avenue and Castleton Boulevard (shown as Osbert Road) were omitted.

The ninth Earl of Scarbrough (1813-84) who projected the development of Skegness as a seaside resort, and his estate agent, Henry Vivian Tippet (1734-1902) who supervised the construction.

SKEGNESS 1905

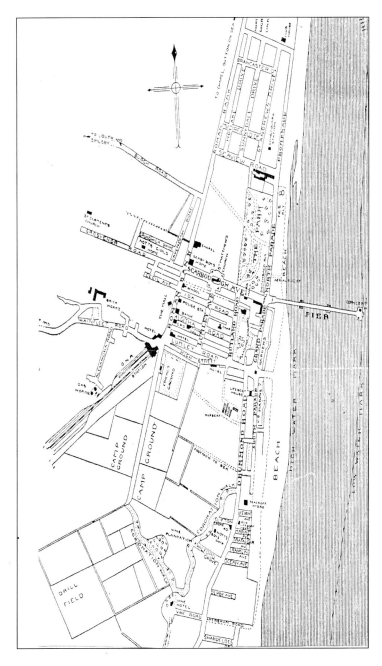

SKEGNESS, 1905.

Half a century on from 1849 and Skegness was a different sort of place entirely, with a population well over two thousand., The ninth Earl of Scarbrough had laid out a model watering place, with parades and pier, a new main shopping street and piped water, gas and sewage disposal. The Great Northern Railway, after enlarging the station five years earlier and doubling the track, was running even more summertime day excursions from the East Midlands towns, as well as London and South Yorkshire.

The Park, near the seafront, was never quite as formal as displayed on the map and soon degenerated into an area of sand dune and masses of sea buckthorn with tall forest trees and pinewoods. It is now all built over with Park Avenue, Glentworth Crescent, and private hotels and residential flats lining North Parade. But in 1905, Castleton Boulevard was still thirty years away and the blank space between the Park and Roman Bank was nearly all grazing land and allotments. South of Lumley Road the even larger space was taken up with nursery gardens and greenhouses, whilst the 'Camp Grounds' were green fields used in summer months by visiting Boys Brigades and other organisations for their annual camps, as well as sites for travelling circuses.

The brickworks shown off Wainfleet Road was supplemented by another on Burgh Road, near the Beacon Way junction, but just off the map, both with tall brick chimneys, with another brickyard on Roman Bank.

Grosvenor Road was only partly surfaced, deteriorating to a cart track before|reaching the old parish church of St. Clement's. Church and cemetery were accessible from Burgh Road by field paths and a rutted cart road known as 'the gatrum,' with several field gates to open along the route.

None of the present County Council Schools were there in 1905, but the National School on Roman Bank, near the Ida Road junction (now Halifax Bank), had been there since 1880, with an Infants School at the Assembly Rooms in High Street, but not shown on the map.

The bank on Roman Bank was the Capital & Counties, but it only occupied a part of what was really the Earl of Scarbrough's Estate Office. Further along, the map shows a Town Hall, although it was always called the Council Offices, occupied by Skegness Urban District Council. In 1922, the Earl and the Council exchanged buildings and the bank vacated the Roman Bank site to move to new premises in Lumley Road, by which time it had become Lloyds Bank.

On the south corner of the Roman Bank-Algitha Road junction was the Post Office (GPO), but it moved to a new building on the other side of Roman Bank in 1929 and the old office eventually became the Trustees Savings Bank, now a branch of Lloyds-TSB.

The Police Station shown on Roman Bank remained there until moving to the present much larger headquarters in Park Avenue in 1974. In Drummond Road, most of the avenues ~leading to the sea were already laid out, many built on with holiday bungalows and houses let during the season, often for long periods, to well-to-do families from the Nottingham, Leicester and Derby areas. The resident population of Skegness at this date was a little less than three thousand.

SKEGNESS 1935

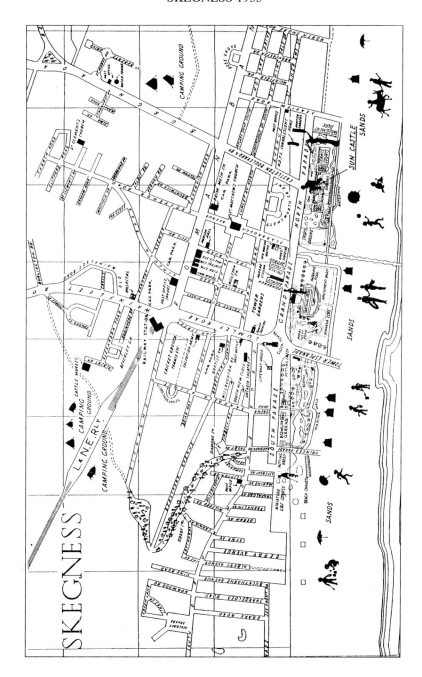

SKEGNESS 1935

By 1935, Skegness Urban District Council had taken over the foreshore from the Earl of Scarbrough and their redevelopment scheme was almost completed. The 1920-30s was a really vital period for the resort, for, in a matter of about fifteen years, it saw it transformed from a small watering place to an important East Coast seaside resort. With the exception of the pier, almost all the holiday amenities, between the parades and the beach, had been added during that period and the majority are still there today.

In 1935, the railway and the motor coach were still the chief means of bringing visitors to the coast, but from the 1950s the motor car took over, with ownership assisted by full employment and the end of petrol rationing following the end of the Second World War.

Back in the 1930s, the pier was still jutting far out into the North Sea with the Victorian entrance reached by a wide stepped entrance from the parade and two broad ramps for bathchairs, perambulators and pedestrians. Tower Esplanade was dominated by the Foreshore Centre, containing the tourism bureau, left luggage office and lost children's shelter, whilst further along was Billy Rowe's jugs of tea kiosk. The lifeboat station, of course, was still on South Parade and the Boating Lake Cafe was about the only other building at that end of the Esplanade.

Between there and the pier was the big open-air Bathing Pool, joined to the Embassy Ballroom and Restaurant by the Orchestral Piazza, a partly sheltered open space with a domed bandstand. The Piazza was utilised for a variety of activities, but was rather underused. The 1928-29 amenities were nearly all demolished in 1999 with only the rebuilt Embassy Centre and the amusement park surviving and the car park next to the parade was built over in 2003.

The map shows wide spaces of undeveloped land, notably in the areas of Beresford Avenue, Richmond Drive, Wainfleet Road and Burgh Road and the Second World War was to intervene before most of it was built on. The Skegness population in 1935 would be about nine and a half thousand.

SKEGNESS COUNCIL CHAIRMEN AND TOWN MAYORS.

Skegness Local Board (Chairmen), 1885-95.

1885-86/87/88	H.E.Iremonger (3).	1888-89/90	G.Dunkley (2).
1888 (2 months.)	H.V.Tippet.	1890-91/92/93/94/95	C.F.Grantham (5).

Skegness Urban District Council (Chairmen), 1895-1974.

1895-96	C.F.Grantham (6).	1930-31	R.J.G. Dutton.
1896-97	A.W.Rowley.	1931-32	F. Cooper.
1897-98	S.G.Randall.	1932-33	J. Crawshaw.
1898-99	J. Barlow.	1933-34	W. Hudson (2).
1899-1900	J. Green.	1934-35	F. Wood (2).
1900-01	F. Kirkby.	1935-36	J. Rawding.
1901-02	S. Moody.	1936-37	F. Cooper (2).
1902-03	G. Dunkley. (3)	1937-38	J. Crawshaw (2).
1903-04	J.G.Middleton.	193839	G.E. Holmes (3)
1904-05	G.H.J. Dutton.	1939-40	W. Hudson (3).
1905-06	A. W. Rowley (2).	1940-41	S. Chester.
1906-07	A.J. Eggleston.	1941-42	F. Wood (3).
1907-08	J. Barlow (2).	1942-43	T.W. West.
1908-09	F. Kirkby (2).	1943-44	G.H. Hannam.
1909-10	S.G.Randall (2).	1944-45	F. Davis.
1910-11	S. Moody (2)	1945-46	J. Crawshaw (3).
1911-12	J.H. Shelley.	1946-47	A. Denham.
1912-13	T. Marshall.	1947-48	A. Corden.
1913-14	G.H. Randall.	1948-49	C.E. Fry.
1914-15	G.F. Ball.	1949-50	R.J.G. Dutton. (2).
1915-16	J.R. Sleight.	1950-51	S. Chester (2).
1916-17	G.E. Holmes.	1951-52	G.F. Swaby.
1917-18	J. Walker.	1952-53	J. Crawshaw (4).
1918-19	W. Clayton.	1953-54	Mrs. E. Barratt.
1919-20	W.P. Moody.	1954-55	A. Denham (2).
1920-21	B. Sweeten.	1955-56	A.E. Thompson.
1921-22	C. Bycroft.	1956-57	L.N. Walthall.
1922-23	S. Moody (3).	1957-58	J.H. Edwards.
1923-24	D.C. Haley.	1958-59	G.F. Swaby (2).
1924-25	W. Hudson.	1959-60	D.H. Lilley.
1925-26	C.T. Jessap.	1960-61	J.D. Williamson.
1926-27	F. Wood.	1961-62	Mrs. E. Barratt (2).
1927-28	H. Thornton.	1962-63	P.J. Tonglet.
1928-29	G.E. Holmes (2)	1963-64	T. Senior.
1929-30	B. Sweeten (2).	1964-65	F.A. Wise.

1965-66	D.R. Hudson.	1970-71	G.F. Walker.
1966-67	Mrs. V. Elwis.	1971-72	J.W. Elliott.
1967-68	Mrs. E. Barratt (3).	1972-73	D.C. Pendrigh.
1968-69	J.N. Pratt.	1973-74	H. Fainlight.
1969-70	R.W. Scott.		

Skegness Town Council (Mayors). 1974- .

1974-75	H. Fainlight (2).	1991-92	R. Sadler.
1975-76	Mrs. E. Barratt (4).	1992-93	R. Scott (4).
1976-77	P.J. Tonglet (2).	1993-94	J.E.Shaw.
1977-78	H. Hall.	1994-95	Mrs. E. Sutton (2).
1978-79	R.W. Scott (2).	1995-96	K.J. Holland (3).
1979-80	D. Sorby.	1996-97	M.C. Anderson.
1980-81	H. Fainlight (3).	1997-98	M. Clark.
1981-82	K. Holland.	1998-99	T. Bryan.
1982-83	J. Forman.	1999-2000	Mrs.S.J. Mackenzie.
1983-84	H. Bayes.	2000-01	F. Grunnill (2).
1984-85	R. Sadler.	2001-02	Mrs. S. Binch.
1985-86	Mrs. N. Fagan.	2002-03	G. Ellis.
1986-87	R.W. Scott (3).	2003-04	A. Fletcher.
1987-88	Mrs. E. Sutton.	2004-05	M.C. Anderson (2).
1988-89	H. Fainlight (4).	2005-06	B. O'Connor.
1989-90	K.J. Holland(2),	2006-07	P.P. Kemp
1990-91	F. Grunnill.		

NOTE. Councillors serving a second or longer terms as chairman or mayor are indicated by the appropriate number in brackets after their names.

Skegness Town Clerks .

1885-95	C.J. Dashper	Part-time, Private Solicitor	Local Board
1895-1922	Tweed, Stephens & Co	Part-time, Private Solicitor	U.D Council
1922-27	W. Frearson	Part-time, Private Solicitor	U.D Council
1927-56	I.M. Cule		U.D Council
1956-74	M. Turner		U.D Council
1974-84	P. Bailey		Town Council
1984-89	D Hill		Town Council
1989-94	R Lloyd-Smith		Town Council
1994-	A. Crawshaw		Town Council

Note: Dates before 1974 are approximate

SKEGNESS TOWN COUNCIL replaced Skegness Urban District Council in the reorganisation of local government in 1974 when Skegness also elected representatives on the new East Lindsey District Council and Lincolnshire County Council.

The Council retained office accommodation in the Town Hall, North Parade, shared with East Lindsey District Council's Skegness sub-office. The Town Council is made up of 20 councillors, five members representing each of the four wards of St. Clements, Scarbrough, Winthorpe and Seacroft. Councillors are elected for a period of four years in elections held every four years. The Town Mayor is appointed by the Council in May, to serve a period of one year.

Skegness is represented by 8 members on East Lindsey District Council (total 60 members) and 2 members on Lincolnshire County Council (total 77 members) The Council in 2005 was awarded Quality Status, the first Town Council in Lincolnshire to achieve this qualification.

HONOURED CITIZENS OF SKEGNESS.

The town's most prestigious award to people who have 'rendered distinguished and valuable service to all the inhabitants of the Town of Skegness' over a period of time. The award, inaugurated by Skegness Town Council in 1979, is in the form of a framed certificate, signed by the Town Mayor and the Town Clerk, and the names of the recipients are engraved on a wood plaque in the Council Chamber, The recipients to date are as follows:

1979	Mrs. E. Barratt, MBE.
1983	A.E. Thompson.
1987	P.J. Tonglet.
1992	Harold Bayes.
1992	Harold Fainlight, MBE.
1993	Cllr. C.W. Scott.
1999	Mrs. E. Sutton.
2001	Winston Kime.
2002	R.F. Sadler.
2003	F. Grunnill.
2005	Cllr. K.J. Holland, BEM.

JOLLY FISHERMAN SILVER STATUETTES.

These have been awarded for many years, at the discretion of the Council Chairman or Town Mayor, in acknowledgement of notable work for the town, esteemed achievements or souvenirs for services rendered.

Skegness Local Government Board, 1887, first elected in 1885 under new government legislation. Standing, left to right: C.Houghton, G.J.Crofts, W.H.Swift, C.J.Dashper (town clerk), Rev.F.Baldwin (hon. treasurer), Col.H.E.Iremonger (chairman, in skull cap), Dr.C.J.Bernard (medical officer of health), E.R.Capon (surveyor), C.Hildred, C.W.Rowley. Seated: F.Cartwright, Charles F.Grantham, E.A.Jackson (assistant town clerk), Geo. Dunkley, S.Clarke, H.V.Tippet, F.L.Wardle.

Skegness Urban District Council, 1922-23. Back row left to right H.Mather (rate collector), W.Clifford (gasworks manager), Wm. Frearson (town clerk), V.H.Tippet (assistant town clerk), R.H.Jenkins (engineer and surveyor), Middle row: Councillors - ?- , -?- , C.T.Jessap, Thos. Marshall, Hedley Thornton, Walter Hudson, J.W.Borman, Frank Wood. S.Vasey (waterworks manager), Seated: Councillors W.Patey Moody, Dr.B.Sweeten, David C.Haley, Samuel Moody (chairman), Charles Bycroft, G.Goodess, Geo.F.Ball.

The last Skegness Urban District Council, 1973-74. Back row left to right G.Tanner (deputy treasurer), K.Griffiths (deputy town clerk), K.Hargreaves (treasurer), M.Turner (town clerk), J.Taylor (engineer and surveyor), H.Haywood (foreshore director), J.T.Ainsworth (chief public health inspector). Middle row: Councillors: E.J.Wright, B.M.Astle, A.Thompson, V.J.Sheehan-Hunt, H.Hall, C.J.Sawyer, Mrs.E.Sutton, D.Sorby. Front row:Councillors D.Hudson, F.A.Wise, Mrs.E.Barrat MBE., Mrs.V.Elwis, H.Fainlight, MBE. (chairman), Dr.D.C.Pendrigh, J.Tonglet, R.Scott, M.Moffat.

Skegness Town Council 2001 - 2002 Back row: Rev. J. Wickstead, (mayor's chaplain), Mrs P.R. Phillips, Mrs R. Amis, N.R. Pimperton, A.Crawshaw (town Clerk). Middle row: P.P. Kemp, B, O'Connor, A.Fletcher, T. Bryan, J.E.Straw, J. Byford, K. Milner. Front row:D.R. Edgington, R.F.Sadler, F. Grunnill, Mrs S. Binch (town mayor), G.O. Ellis (deputy mayor), K.J. Holland B.E.M., I.L. Cameron. Not present: M.Clark, M.C.Anderson, Mrs S.J. MacKenzie.

The Council Offices, 29, Algitha Road, occupied by the newly-formed Skegness Urban District Council in 1895. In 1920 the Earl of Scarbrough sold his Estate Office, on the corner of Roman Bank and Algitha Road, to the SUDC and moved to their former building at No.29, Algitha Road.

The Council Offices, Roman Bank, originally the Scarbrough Estate Office, purchased by Skegness UDC in 1920.

The Roman Bank Council Offices, almost totally destroyed by fire in 1928, reopened in 1931, as shown above. It was distinguished from the original exterior chiefly by the open balcony above the main entrance, half hidden here by a tree. The balcony was used to announce election results and other proclamations. The building was demolished soon after the Council moved to North Parade in 1964. The fire station can be seen far left.

The National Deposit Friendly Society Convalescent Home was opened in 1927 and became the Town Hall when purchased by Skegness UDC in 1964. East Lindsey District Council took it over in 1974, with accommodation for Skegness Town Council. Pictured here in the 1930s

INDEX.

Some items are grouped together under subjects, e.g. Lawn Theatre under 'Cinemas and Theatres.' These subject headings are as follows:

Amusements Parks.
Banks.
Car Parks.
Churches.
Cinemas and Theatres.
Convalescent Homes.
Football.

Golf.
Hotels.
Railways.
Royalty.
Schools.
Sewerage.
Streets.

The word, 'Skegness,' beginning any title, for the most part is ignored and is indexed under the next descriptive word. Where street names are used only as locations they are not indexed.

Addlethorpe. 31
Advancement Association. 40, 53, 77
Aero Club. 37, 49
Aerodromes. 49
Agricultural Shows. 25, 28, 35
Agricultural Workers' Rallies. 49, 52
Air displays and flights. 26, 30, 35, 37
Air Raid Precautions (ARP). 42, 43
Air raid shelters. 45
Air Training Corps. 47
Alford. 12, 15, 20, 21, 45, 68, 73, 75
Alhambra Skating Rink. 28
Allan, Elizabeth. 41, 68
Alpha Club. 68
Amusement Parks:
    Butlin's. See under 'Butlin's.'
    North Parade. 34
    Pleasureland. 30, 34, 41
Angling Club. 56
Ansthruther House. 68
Argos catalogue shop. 73
Athletic Club. 55
Attenborough, Sir David. 61
Attlee, Clement. 49
Avenue Club. 23
Avery, John. 12
Axenstrasse. 35
Azah sinking. 25

Badminton Club. 60
Baker's Oven. 66
Baldwin, Rev. F. 10, 11, 15, 16, 91
Ball, Geo. F. 30, 41, 88, 91

Bamber, H. 35, 37
Banana Brigade. 44
bands. 32, 38, 40, 49
bandstand. 42
Bank Holidays. 13, 20, 25, 26, 31, 33, 40, 54
Banks:
    Capital & Counties. 11, 21, 25, 85
    Garfitts. 11
    Lloyds-TSB. 22, 25, 85
    Midland (HSBC). 28
    National Westminster. 12
Barnes, Sid. 31
barrow boys. 51
Bateman's Brewery. 35, 40
bathing machines. 6
bathing pools and baths. See *'swimming pools.'*
Batley, Robert 20, 24, 25
Battle of Flowers. 20
beach nourishment. 71
Beacon Medical Practice. 76
Beeching Plan. 57, 60
Berry family. 20, 29, 62
Bevan, Aneurin. 52
birching offence. 31
Birks, Alan. 61
births and deaths. 11, 15
Blizzard, The Great. 54
Boating Club. 59
Boating Lake. 30, 35, 73, 87
bombing, wartime. 45, 46, 48, 51, 53, 62
Booth, General Bramwell. 29
Boots Chemists. 33, 70

Borman family. 12, 18
Boston. 8, 13, 18, 26, 29, 38, 43, 46, 50, 53, 54, 55, 58, 59, 60
Boston & Skegness Parliamentary Division. 65
Bosworth. W.G. 53
Botton Bros. 58
bowls. 38
Boys Brigade. 20, 24, 33, 85
Boy Scouts. 24, 40
boxing. 49
brickworks. 11, 46, 51, 53, 63, 65, 85
British Legion, Royal. 72
Broughton, Rowland. 59
Buffaloes (RAOB). 33, 48
Burgh-le-Marsh. 6, 15, 16, 26, 51, 73
Business & Professional Women's Club. 68
buses. 29, 39
Butlin's:
    airfield. 49
    amusement parks. 32, 34, 41, 49, 57, 58
    bus stations. 63
    Butlin House. 60
    carnivals. 38
    fires. 43, 61
    Gaiety Theatre. 73
    Holiday Camp. 40, 41, 42, 43, 50, 59, 61, 63, 68, 70
    Mablethorpe. 41
    royal visitors. 50, 59, 70
Butlin, Sir William. 41, 62, 64

Cafe Dansant. *See under 'Foreshore Centre.'*
camels. 65
Campbell, Sir Malcolm. 31
carnivals. 38
Car Parks and Coach Stations:
    Arcadia. 68
    Central. 32, 87
    Lawn. 48, 67, 68
    Pier Field. 47, 53
    Richmond Drive. 63, 68
    Scarbrough Avenue. 53
carriers. 6
Cash. G.H. 15
Casino, The. 28, 46, 95
Cast Stone Works, Skegness. 63
cattle markets. 10, 30, 41, 45
CCTV detection. 75
cemetery. 66
Central Hall. *See under 'Cinemas and Theatres.'*
Chamberlain, Neville. 32, 43
Chapel St. Leonards. 47, 50, 59
Choral Society. 21
Chrysanthemum Society. 42
church attendance. 7
Churches:
    Baptist. 16, 17, 24, 29, 33, 71
    Methodist, Primitive. 7, 11, 19, 63
    Methodist, Wesleyan. 6, 7, 9, 12, 19, 46, 63, 73
    Roman Catholic. 18, 51
    Salvation Army. 25, 29, 35, 40, 71, 72
    Seacroft. 51
    St. Clements. 6, 7, 39, 56, 66, 67, 85
    St. Matthew's. 10, 15, 16, 17, 19, 22, 30, 38, 42
    St. Paul's Free Church. 16
    Winthorpe St. Mary's. 6, 7, 26, 63, 66
Church Farm Museum. 62
church halls. 26, 33, 46, 56, 64
Church Lads' Brigade. 25
Cinemas and Theatres:
    Arcadia Theatre. 24, 34, 42, 60, 66, 68
    Central Hall and Cinema. 24, 38
    Embassy Theatre and Centre. 34, 52, 65, 75, 76, 87
    Gaiety Theatre. 73
    Kings Theatre and Cinema. 33, 42, 53
    Lawn Theatre and Cinema. 24, 28, 39
    Parade Cinema. 38, 54, 62
    Pier Theatre. 50, 59
    Tower Theatre and Cinema. 28, 46, 51
circus. 39
Citizens' Advice Bureau. 71
Civic Society. 5, 66, 75
Clark, Cllr.M. 76
Clark, Samuel. 11, 14
Cleethorpes. 16

Clemence, Ray. 67
Clements, Fred. 20, 24, 28, 34
Clock Tower. 19, 46, 47, 56, 67, 72
coal landings and merchants. 6, 81
coastguards. 7, 10, 55, 64
coat-of-arms. Inside front cover, 57
Cobham, Sir Alan. 35,
Combined Ex-Services Assocn. 72
Compass Gardens.35, 52, 69, 72
Convalescent Homes:
    Carey House. 38, 52, 71
    Derbyshire Miners'. 34
    NDFS. 32, 34, 45, 47, 57, 95
    Nottinghamshire Miners'. 38, 63
    Seely House. 52, 63
Co-operative Societies. 19, 24, 33, 65, 71 , 76
Coronation Walk. 21, 46
Council of Christian Churches. 40
Council Offices. *See under 'Town Halls.'*
coursing, rabbit. 21
courthouses and magistrates. 16, 23, 31, 35, 61, 64, 73
Cow Club. 16
Crawshaw family. 14, 15, 29, 77, 88
crematorium. 58
Cricket Ground. 10, 18, 22, 64
cricket matches. 15, 31, 36, 40, 43
Croft. 16, 31
Crofts family. 18, 21, 66, 91
Crowson, Mrs.J. 69
Customs and Excise. 21
cycling. 11, 18, 22, 37
cycleway. 73

Daniels, Paul. 68
Davidson, Rev. Harold. 41
Day Centre. 66
Deaf Association. 35
Deans Farm. 46
Decimal Day. 60
Defence Zone (Wartime). 44
DeMond, Henri. 28
Derbyshire Children's Seaside Home. 71, 74
Derbyshire Miners' Holiday Centre. 43, 50, 54, 68

development plans .9, 28, 31, 35, 82, 87
Disbrowe, Rev.C.P. 18, 19
divers (pier). 50
Dixons store. 66
Dobson, Helen. 69
Dodsworth, H.L. 38.
dovecote. 66
Drainage Boards. 68, 75
drugs. 21
Dunn family. 17, 18
Dunkley family. 7, 9, 13, 14, 18, 20, 25, 88, 91
Dutton's Cash Stores. 57, 88
Dwyer, Ted. 59

East Coast Flood, 1953. 52
East Lindsey District Council. 61, 67, 74, 76, 90, 95
East Lindsey Parliamentary Division. 65
Edinburgh Woollen Mill. 73
elections. 14, 21
electricity supply. 37
Eliza museum ship. 12, 25
Elsie, Lily. 26
Enderby, Matthew. 10
Epton's Corner. 31
Epton, R.J. 16, 31
Etam. 57
Europa disaster. 27
evacuees, wartime. 44
Everington family. 9, 11

Fainlight, Harold. MBE. 61, 62, 69, 72, 75, 89, 90, 92
fairgrounds. *See 'amusement parks.'*
Fairy Dell Pool. 33, 35
Festival Centre. 51, 57
Fields, Gracie. 42
Figure 8 Switchback. 14, 23, 25, 60
fires. 33, 36, 43, 50, 57, 61, 64, 95
Fire Service. 13, 60
Firsby Junction. *See 'Railways.'*
fishing. 18
Fletcher, A.E. 24, 28,, 48
floods. *See 'Storms and Floods.'*
Flower Lovers Club. 56

98

Football:
   Clubs - Blue Rovers. 43
   early clubs. 11, 20, 21
   Thursday. 43, 48
   Town. 48, 50, 54, 55
   United. 43, 62
   competitions. 20, 21, 43, 55
   grounds. 11, 55, 62, 75
   matches. 18, 54
Foreshore Centre. 24, 27, 29, 39, 60, 85
foreshore leases and sales. 18, 29, 35
foreshore staff. 38, 53
Forum, Skegness. 66, 72
fountains.15, 33
Frearson, Raymond. 31, 36
Freeman, Hardy & Willis. 72
Freemasons. 11
Friskney. 9, 71
Frith's Restaurant. 28
Fry, C.B. 32
Fry, Cedric. 30, 88

Gadsby pier divers. 50
Gardiner, H.S. 52
gas masks. 42, 44
Gas Showrooms. 39, 73
gasworks. 9, 27, 37
Gateway supermarket. 68
Gerard capture. 26
German gun. 36
Gibraltar Point. 6, 7, 17, 19, 38, 43, 44, 46,
   50, 52,53, 54, 55, 57, 60, 61, 66, 74
Gibson, Guy. 45
Giles, James. 39, 42
Girl Guides. 59
Gladstone, W.E. 19
Gleitze, Mercedes. 35
Golf:
   North Shore. 23, 24, 63, 73
   Seacroft 18, 45
Grandways supermarket. 64, 67
Granny's Opening. 23
Grantham. 43, 67
Grantham, Chas.F. 13, 14, 18, 20, 23,
   88, 91
grapefruit salvage. 49

gravestone recording. 67
Greenwood's Cafe. 41
Greenwoods Menswear. 57
Greetham family. 29, 33, 51, 64, 65
Grimsby. 41, 44, 60, 61
Grunnill family. 17, 25, 27, 89, 90, 93

Hall, The. 66, 68, 72, 80
Harding, Gilbert. 53
Hassall, John. *See under 'Jolly Fisherman.'*
Henshall, L.J. 37
Herald, Skegness. 12, 19, 20, 58
Hildred family. 6, 9, 11, 14, 81, 91
Hildreds, The. 67, 68, 70
Hill, Benny. 54
Historical Association. 59, 61
hockey. 31, 36
Hogsthorpe. 12
Holland, K.J. 64, 89, 90, 93
Home Guard. 44
Honoured Citizens. 90
Horncastle. 20, 30
Horncastle Parliamentary Division. 14, 65
horse racing. 30, 39
horses and carts. 55
Horticultural Society. 16
hospitals. 25, 29, 43, 50, 51, 56, 64
Hoteliers' Association. 41
Hotels, Inns and Public Houses:
   Charnwood Tavern. 8
   County Hotel. 40
   Crown Hotel. 70
   Dorchester Hotel. 14
   Grosvenor House Hotel. 14, 35, 46
   Hildreds Hotel. 6, 19, 39, 67, 68,
      80, 81
   Lion Hotel. 11, 16, 20, 22, 65
   Lumley Hotel.10, 11, 15, 67, 71, 72
   Marine Hotel. 74
   New Hotel. *See 'Hildreds Hotel.'*
   Pier Hotel. 11, 57
   Red House Hotel. 47, 62
   Red Lion Hotel. *See 'Lion Hotel.'*
   Seacroft Hotel. 46
   Seaview Hotel. 7, 11, 14, 26, 37
   Shades Hotel. 67

Ship Hotel. 6, 21, 40, 80, 81
temperance hotels. 6
Vine Hotel. 6, 21, 35
Welcome Inn. 54
housing. 29, 48, 67, 68, 70, 81
hoverboat trips. 59
Hucks, B.C. 26
Hudson, Richard. 17
Hungarian Rising, 1956. 54
Hunstanton. 13, 35

Iceland supermarket. 67, 71
illuminations. 37, 52
Industrial estate. 55, 56, 74
Ingoldmells. 7, 12, 29, 49, 52, 59, 63, 65, 68, 69, 70, 71
Ingram, Herbert. 8

Jacksons Corner. 8, 43
Janice Sutton Dance School. 75, 76
Jazz Club. 54
Jenkins, Rowland H. 28, 30, 33, 91
Joel, Arthur. 39
Jolly Fisherman poster. 23, 27, 30, 40, 50, 57, 68, 69, 72, 74, 77
Jolly Fisherman Satuettes. 90
Joywheel. 27
Jungle, The. *See 'The Park.'*

KFC restaurant. 73
Kimberley House. 47
King George V Walk. 61
Kwik Save supermarket. 71

Lagoon Walk. 63, 64, 67
Larwood, Harold. 36
laundries. 9, 30
lavatories, public. 18, 21, 39
Lawrence, D.H. 21
libraries. 12, 15, 35, 36, 49, 51
licences. 21, 26
Lidl supermarket. 76
lifeboats. 6, 8, 25, 31, 37, 42, 47, 48
Lifeboat Guild. 56
lifeboat, inshore. 58

lifeboat, first motor. 37
lifeboat stations. 6. 8. 59. 69. 87
lifeboat tractor. 32
lifeline, mortar-fired. 6
Lill family. 29, 63
Lincoln. 5, 9, 30
Lincs. Coast Shipwreck Assocn. 6, 8
Lincolnshire County Council. 33, 61, 90
Lincolnshire Road Car Co. 39, 69
Lindsey County Council. 16, 50, 55
Lions Club. 62
Lipton's Stores. 57
Local Board. 14, 15, 18, 91
Louth. 60, 61, 68, 75
Lovat Scouts Regt. 26
Lyndhurst Social Club. 19

Mablethorpe. 47, 50, 71
Major family. 24, 25, 58, 73
Manby, Capt. G. 6
Marine Gardens. 15, 29, 32, 33
marine walks. 50, 62, 63, 64, 67, 70, 73
Marks & Spencer. 41
marriages. 11
Martin-Simpson, Mrs.L. 26
Massingberd, C.B. 6
Methodist Church Circuit. 73
Millennium First College. 76
minefields. 48
miniature railway. 71
Moat House, The. 79
Monson, Lord. 6
Moody family. 6, 11, 13, 18, 23, 88, 91
Morris, Canon A.H. 39. 54
motorboat, first. 25
motorcar, first. 20
motor cycling. 31
motor races. 23, 30, 31
Murphy Radio. 52, 56
museums. 39, 42, 62

Nationwide. 66
Natureland. 58, 69
nature reserves. 9, 50, 52, 55, 57, 60, 66, 74

News, Skegness. 58, 66
North Bracing. 50
North Shore sea walk. 73
Nottingham. 9, 12, 19, 23, 28, 33, 36, 42, 51, 56, 57, 85
Nottingham Forest FC.18
Nottinghamshire Boys' Holiday Home. 33
Nottinghamshire Girls' Holiday Home. 58

Observer Corps. 44
Old Age Pension. 24
Old Folks' Treat. 21
One-way streets. 56, 75
Operatic Society. 29, 58

Panda's Palace. 67
Panton butchers. 65
parish chest. 14
Parish Hall. See 'Church Halls.'
Parish Magazine. 11
Parish Register. 14
Parish Vestry. 12, 13, 15, 16, 17
Park, The. 20, 32, 34, 65, 85
parliamentary divisions. 14, 65
Parochial Church Council. 63, 70
Parry-Thomas, J.C. 31
passive resistance. 22
Pensioners' Hall. 50, 58
Pier. 9, 10, 13, 24, 27, 40, 41, 44, 45, 49, 56, 59, 60, 63, 66, 87
Pig Club. 8, 26, 54
pigeon shooting. 11
Player, John D. 27
Playgoers Society. 41, 73
Playing Fields. 49, 69, 71
Pleasureland. 30
Pleasure Gardens. See 'Tower Gardens.'
Police. 12, 13, 28, 46, 61, 75, 85
Polka, The Skegness. 14
population. 78
Porter,Abraham. 10
postcodes. 60
Post Office. 22, 35, 71, 76, 85
Pottery, Skegness. 62
Powell, Enoch. 56

Prince Edward Walk. 70
Probus Club. 61

RAF Recruit Centre. 46
Railways:
  Beeching Plan. 57
  Boston. 22
  diesel trains. 53
  East Lincs. Railway. 60
  excursions. See 'trippers.'
  Firsby Junction. 11, 20, 60
  Great Northern Rly. 8, 11, 18, 20, 22, 25, 30, 58, 77, 85
  Havenhouse. 20
  Kirkstead Junction. 25
  Lincoln. 9, 22, 25
  London & North Eastern Rly. 30, 43
  Midland Rly. 22
  Seacroft. 20, 53
  South Curve (Firsby). 11
  station. 8, 58, 65, 69
  Wainfleet. 8
Ramblers Association. 71
Randall family. 9, 12, 18, 88
Rank-Bush-Murphy factory. 56
Rankin, Miss M.E. 27
Raynor, George. 55
Reading Room. 12
recesslon. 13
Rectors. 10, 11
refuse removal. 20, 70
Reynardson, Chas. 6
Richmond Leisure Centre. 35, 70
RNLI. 8
Robey, George. 42
Robin Hood Rifles. 19
Roche Abbey Quarry. 9
Rock and Roll. 54
rock manufacture. 56
roller coasters. See 'Switchbacks.'
Rollinson, Capt. W.A. 30
Rose engineering works. 53, 68
Round Table. 51
Rowe family. 39, 49, 85
Rowley family. 14, 18, 88, 91

101

Royal Air Force Assocn. 49
Royal Arthur, HMS. 44, 45, 47, 68
Royal British Legion. 49
Royal Observer Corps. 44
Royalty:
   coronations. 21, 25, 52
   jubilees. 14, 19
   marriages. 17
Royal visits:
   Duchess of Gloucester. 43, 71
   Duke of Edinburgh. 10, 50
   Duke of Gloucester. 74
   Prince Edward. 70
   Prince of Wales. 60
   Princess Margaret. 59
   Princess Marie Louise. 32
   Princess Royal. 57
Rugby Club. 50

Safeway supermarket. 70
St. John's Ambulance Brigade. 31, 59
Sands Pavilion. *See Foreshore Centre*
Sayers' Jewellery. 74
Scarbrough, Countess of. 10, 19, 85
Scarbrough, Earls of. 6, 9, 10, 11, 12, 13, 14, 15, 17, 18, 20, 24, 25, 27, 28, 29, 40, 55, 57, 66, 68, 82, 83, 85, 94
Schools:
   Brythwen High School. 19
   Earl of Scarbrough`High. 67, 68
   Grammar. 38, 69, 70
   Infants. 23, 58, 74, 85
   Junior. 40, 71, 72
   Lumley Secondary. 37, 67, 71, 72
   Morris Secondary. 54, 67
   National. 10, 16, 18, 23, 37
   Richmond Primary. 62
   Roman Bank. 6
   Seacroft Preparatory 46, 51
   Seacroft Special for Girls. 51
   Seathorne Primary. 52
   Winthorpe. 8, 52
scooter rally. 66
Sea Cadets. 47
Seacroft Fields. 67

Seagull Conservation. 69
seals. 53
Searby family. 31, 36
Sea Scouts. 59, 71
Sewerage:
   Cowbank. 9, 23
   disposal costs. 20
   Ingoldmells. 59, 65
   Middlemarsh. 38, 59, 65, 70
Shannon disaster. 17
sheep clipping. 9
sheepdog trials. 41
shrimping. 11
skateboarding. 69
skating rinks. 28, 37
Skegness 2000. 66
Skegness Motor Service (SMS). 29, 39
Skegness Society. 25
Smuggling. 8, 21
Somerfield supermarket. 76
South Bracing. 50
Specsavers opticians. 72
Spendlove, K.G. 38
Spilsby. 6, 8, 9, 10, 15, 20, 21, 22, 23, 51, 59, 61, 64, 67
Sports Centre. 68
sprat shoal. 59
Standard, Skegness. 28, 64
Stanhope, Edward. 14
Steamboat Co. and steamers. 13, 24
Steere, Rev. E. 7
Stickney. 20
Stiebels lace factory. 56
Stiffkey. 41
storm and flood. 6, 11, 23, 29, 31, 36, 44, 47, 50, 52, 54, 63, 68, 75
street lighting. 9, 51
Streets:
   Alexandra Road. 11, 13
   Berry Way. 62
   Burgh Road. 26, 87
   Castleton Boulevard. 39, 82
   Drummond Road. 47
   Edinburgh Avenue. 10
   Glentworth Crescent. 45, 85

Grand Parade. 9, 13, 46, 47
Grosvenor Road. 85
Heath Road. 55
High Street. 13, 48, 56, 72
Lincoln Road. 56
Lumley Avenue. 46, 47
Lumley Road. 9. 13. 14. 31. 36. 42. 46. 48. 54. 56. 75
Lumley Square. 15, 37, 73
North Parade. 29, 45, 46, 47, 85
Norwood Road. 45
Park Avenue. 45, 47
Prince Alfred Avenue. 10
Prince George Street. 56
Richmond Drive. 10, 45, 87
Roman Bank.26, 32
Rutland Road. 13
Saxby Avenue. 40
Scarbrough Avenue. 35, 47
Scarbrough Esplanade. 42
Seacroft Esplanade. 26, 35
Sea View Road. 13
South Parade. 13, 21
Tower Esplanade. 28, 30, 46, 87
Vine Road. 47
Wainfleet Road. 13, 81, 87
Warth Lane. 36
Wilford Grove. 26
Sun Castle. 27, 37, 52
Sunday trading. 34, 37, 72
Sutton Court. 68, 70, 81
Sutton-on-Sea. 12, 47, 50
Swimming Club. 34
Swimming pools.
   Indoor Pool. 68
   Outdoor pools. 33, 68, 75, 87
   Scarbrough Avenue Baths. 12, 33, 42, 53
Switchback. 14, 25

Tapsell, Sir Peter. 65
taxis. 23, 51
Teddy Boys. 54
telephones. 21, 59, 67
television region. 62
tennis. 36

Territorial Army. 26, 31
Theatres. *See 'Cinemas and Theatres.'*
Thimbleby family. 9
Thrall's Garage. 28
Tippett, H.V. 13, 14, 16, 83, 91
Tourism Centres. 60, 75
Tower Gardens. 6, 9, 29, 31, 44, 52, 76
Tower Gardens Pavilion. 10, 21, 29, 42, 46
Tower Row. 31
Town Clerks. 89
Town Council. 61, 74, 90, 95
Town Hall and Council Offices. 11, 27, 32, 33, 36, 52, 57, 58, 61, 77, 85, 90, 94, 95
town twinning. 63
traffic lights. 39
Tramway,- Steam. 12
'travellers.' 76
trippers. 9, 12, 16, 20, 22, 38

Urban District Council. 18, 27, 29, 31, 32, 41, 48, 55, 61, 64, 90, 91, 94, 95

verger. 39
Volunteers, Skegness. 14
votes, parliamentary. 8, 27

wages. 20. 31
Wainfleet. 8, 9, 21, 24, 31, 35, 38, 51, 70, 73, 74
Wainfleet by-pass. 70
Walker, Fredk.W. 29, 35
walking races. 30, 55, 56
ward electoral system. 41
war memorials. 30, 32, 34
Wash Speedway. 38
Wash swim. 35, 61
Warth & Dunkley. 9
water supply. 24, 32, 58, 64
Waterway, 36, 42
Welton-le-Marsh. 24, 32
Whale Museum. 10, 20
whales ashore. 15, 47, 54, 58, 66, 73
Williams, Charlie. 55
Willoughby. 12
Willoughby de Eresby, Lord. 20, 21

Wingate, Joseph. 12, 13, 20
Winter Gardens. 37, 39, 42, 56
Winthorpe. 6, 8, 21, 26, 31, 32, 34, 40, 48, 52, 61, 78, 90
wireless stations. 33, 44
Wise. F.A. 57, 58, 88, 92
Women's Institute. 52
Women's Voluntary Service. 42
Woodside Holiday Camp. 38, 54, 64
Woolworth's stores. 34
Working Men's Club. 33, 48
Wrate's Photography. 65

Yacht Pond, Model. 35
Yarborough, Earl of. 30
Yeadon, John. 58
YMCA Holiday Camps. 28, 38, 54, 64

Zeppelins. 36, 41